WEALTH RIBBON
TAIWAN BOUND, AMERICA BOUND

By brenda Lin

UNIVERSITY OF INDIANAPOLIS PRESS
2004

"Mao Dun" was first published in *Fourth Genre* (vol. 4, no. 2, Fall 2002, Michigan State University Press).

"Umbilical Cord" was first published in *Full Circle Journal: A Journal of Poetry and Prose* (online issue #7, vol.1, Fall 2003).

Although editorial style generally calls for non-English words and phrases to be typeset in italic, the editors of *Wealth Ribbon* chose to use roman type throughout to represent the fluid vocabulary of the multilingual author.

Planning: Phylis Lan Lin, Executive Director, University of Indianapolis Press

Cover design and layout: Jeannine Allen
Chinese painting, cover: Collection of Phylis Lan Lin
Editors: Stephanie Seifert, Erling Peterson, David Noble, Peter Noot

University of Indianapolis Press Advisory Board (2003-2005):
Shirley Bigna, Phylis Lan Lin, David Noble, Peter Noot, Philip Young

Printed in the United States of America

09 08 07 06 05 04   10 9 8 7 6 5 4 3 2 1

ISBN: 0-880938-54-4

Published by
University of Indianapolis Press
University of Indianapolis
1400 East Hanna Avenue
Indianapolis, IN 46227-3697

Fax: (317) 788-3480
E-mail: lin@uindy.edu
http://www.uindy.edu/universitypress

This book is dedicated to my mother.

CONTENTS

MAO DUN

My father once told me this story when I was growing up in Taipei:

A long time ago, there was a street vendor who hollered loudly on street corners to advertise his products. He sold only two things: mao (spears) and dun (shields).

"Come everyone!" the vendor yelled earnestly. "Come and buy my mao! These are the best you will ever find because my mao can spear through anything!" He paused. Then he said, "And you won't believe the superior quality of my dun! These are the most powerful dun; nothing in the world could ever pierce through them!"

A passerby who had heard the vendor's cries stopped before him and asked, "What would happen if you took your mao to your dun?"

In Chinese, my father taught me, mao dun is a phrase that describes a feeling. I was still quite young then, but I didn't need him to specify what that feeling was. When my father delivered the last line of the story, I had already seen a clear image in my mind of the street vendor's face, stunned by the passerby's question, recognizing for the first time that he was selling a contradiction. He looked helplessly at his mao in one hand and his dun in the other and, with measure, brought his all-powerful mao to his indestructible dun. I had to shut my mind's eye because I was afraid of seeing what would actually happen if the two met in forceful collision. Like the mao dun vendor, I believed that his spears could pierce through anything; I also believed that his shields could defend against anything. But how could both of these claims be true?

When I looked up at my father, I remember I felt a great sense of relief. I was relieved because I knew this emotion. I knew how my chest filled with anxiety every time I realized that I put stock in two beliefs that seemingly could not coexist. And yet, for all the times I had sold my own proverbial mao and dun, I never knew the word for that writhing sensation in my mind. I never knew that feeling was even describable. Until then, I had thought feeling mao dun was something I would outgrow. I had thought that with age, I would gather enough information and knowledge to come to know that, in fact, the mao could not destroy everything or the dun was not indestructible. Finally, it would always be one or the other, and never both.

The power of language—of giving names to things, ideas, and emotions—is so essential to our cognition that if nameless, a thing does not exist. Without its signifier, the signified is nothing. And until the day my father taught me the meaning of mao dun, I treated those feelings that brewed within me as if they were nothing. In fact, ignoring those feelings (just as I had immediately turned away from the mao dun vendor at his moment of recognition) had become so habitual that it wasn't until I left home to go to school in the States that I recalled this phrase. It wasn't until I had come to a place where I had to search for an approximate translation of mao dun that I remembered to give name to this feeling that perfectly and poetically described how I felt every day about almost everything.

When I was seventeen, I left my parents in Taiwan to go to school in a small town in upstate New York. I left home with two matching suitcases—a gift from my mother—knowing that for the next few years, I would take the sixteen-hour flight home only once a year. I left home to go to school halfway across the world the same way my brother, Alex, had three years before and the same way all my friends were doing that blazing hot summer after our senior year at the American school in Taipei. Most of us had been born in the States in the 1970s when the United States decided to recognize the Chinese Communists over the Nationalists in Taiwan as the rightful government of China at large. Both sides of my parents' families followed the many Taiwanese who rushed to America to get their green cards and American passports; they had all been uncertain of Taiwan's future. It had been clear then that becoming American was the antidote to Taiwan being infected with, and eventually taken over, by Chinese Communism.

We lived in a house in south San Francisco in the late 1970s, something which had been inconceivable to me when my mother told me about those years in America. In Taipei, there was no space for houses—more than twenty million people lived on our tiny island, about the same population as in all of Australia. My fragmented memories of that house remain at floor level: the brown carpet outside the kitchen; pine needles gathered in a small pyramid in the backyard; the neighbor's dog's wet, black, twitching nose. We left America when I was three or four. My grandparents, aunts, uncles, and cousins all stayed. Only a handful of the people who left Taiwan in the '70s returned—people like my parents and my classmates' parents. But they sent us to the American school, realizing how increasingly important it was to know English. The summer after our senior year, my friends and I often cried, knowing that life was about to change drastically now that we were going to be separated, attending different colleges and universities across the United States. But we also relished this sense of being on the brink of something completely new and exciting. We were seventeen- and eighteen-year-olds, wanting and not wanting to leave home.

Late in August, my parents flew with me to New York. We rented a car and drove north along broad, multilaned highways. My father stepped on the gas, and we sped ahead toward distant mountains covered with tiny trees like many heads of broccoli. Some trees were already turning colors in sudden pockets of oranges and yellows, and my mother sighed at the beautiful scenery as she placed her pale hand on my father's tanned, freckled arm—a signal for him to slow down. In Taipei, there was always too much traffic for anyone to drive very fast. Once, my father woke up extra early for a golf game and drove alone at ninety miles an hour down the empty, blue streets in the predawn half light. He came home with a ticket.

The university I was to attend was perched high on a hill with perfectly kept lawns and old stone buildings. It was apparent to us that the school had little to do with the town over which it sat. Down there, at the bottom of the hill, was a small, desolate town with shop windows that reflected the lonesomeness of an Edward Hopper painting—a lonesomeness that I thought particularly American. Taiwan, I felt, was much too small and crowded a place to know about real loneliness. There was one intersection at the center of town. The stoplight hung from a thick black wire. It bobbed up and down and swayed back and forth when big, long trucks drove through the intersection. There were a few restaurants along the main road, one of which was a Chinese takeout called Main Moon, where my father insisted on having lunch.

The three of us sat down at one of the two tables—the kind with rusted steel legs that could be folded under—and while my mother and I tried not to put our elbows on the sticky surface of the table, my father asked loudly in Chinese what Main Moon's specialties were. The chef behind the counter had a thin face, small eyes, and a rather dark complexion for a Chinese man. He asked us where we came from and then apologized that he could only make do with the ingredients he had. Behind him, in the kitchen filled with oversized chrome appliances, stood a young woman and two young men. We learned that they were family; they had come from Hunan Province in southern China. The older man, the one who spoke with my father, was the uncle, and he turned his head to say something to his nephews in the Hunan dialect. Immediately, they started chopping and throwing vegetables into a black wok that had been heating on the stove. I heard the familiar sahhhhhh sound that I would hear when my mother scooped up vegetables with her hands and dropped them into her wok at home. She would release her rounded hands in an outward motion, like a big ball filled with confetti. The girl, who looked about my age, went and stood by the telephone on the counter. She leaned her cheek into her hand and looked at me, neither curious nor indifferent. When the phone rang, I heard her say into the phone, "May moo watchoo wah." (Main Moon, what do you want?) I wondered whether she understood what she was saying or if the phrase had become like song lyrics that I could not make out and for which I would come up with my own syllabic approximations. After a while, my nonsensical (but melodically accurate) version of the song was the only one I would know, and it hardly mattered what the real lyrics were or what they meant. I supposed "may moo watchoo wah" was just as good as—if not better than—"Main Moon, what do you want" because, though it sounded like mumbo jumbo to someone else, the phrase made perfect sense to her.

When our lunch was ready, the uncle came out from under the counter and brought it to us himself. He smiled at us modestly, backing away and nodding his head, then ducking underneath the counter again and reappearing on the other side. Our lunch was a plate of fried noodles; a bowl of egg drop soup; and a heaping plate of broccoli sautéed with flimsy, canned mushrooms. In Chinese, broccoli is mei guo hua cai, American flower vegetable. As we ate, my father chuckled. I knew he was laughing because the food wasn't very good. He felt sorry that this was the kind of Chinese food I would have for the next four years. After he paid the bill, my father thanked the small Hunan family and said to them as he put his arm around me, "Please, take care of my daughter!" The uncle laughed and said of course, of course, and his gaze moved from my father's face down to mine. I looked away. How could a family whose English vocabulary was limited to items on a take-out menu help me?

After lunch, my parents came with me to my dorm. Across the hall, there was another Chinese family helping their daughter move in. The RA had written our names in magic markers on different colored construction paper and stuck it on our doors. The girl's name was Minnie Keh. She was small, about my size, and wore a pink T-shirt under light blue denim overalls. She had a long face, a pointy nose, and a small, tight mouth. We knew from her last name that she was Taiwanese. Keh was the Taiwanese pronunciation of the Chinese family name Kuo. My father dropped my suitcases and immediately bounded across the hall to introduce himself to the Kehs. They were from Connecticut and had lived there since the '70s. I stood next to my parents as they laughed and talked loudly in Taiwanese with Mr. and Mrs. Keh, noting that Minnie and I were probably the only Taiwanese students they'd seen on the entire campus. My father asked if they'd eaten at Main Moon yet. (They hadn't.) Then he said to Minnie—in English because she clearly did not understand what the parents were saying—"Now you two can take good care of each other!" Minnie glared at me with her narrow eyes, and I tried to smile, but I felt already that I had nothing in common with this girl who had grown up in the suburbs of Connecticut and who probably hated it every time her parents spoke to her in Chinese. I was embarrassed when my parents then turned to say to me in Chinese, "Let's go see your room."

There were two beds in the room; one of them already had a black duffel bag and an unrolled comforter on it. My father helped hoist my suitcases onto the naked plastic mattress of the other bed. On the desk in what had become my side of the room was a sheet of paper listing the events of that day's orientation. In an hour, there was going to be an ice cream mixer on the quad for first-years and their parents. In an hour, my parents would already be on their way back to New York City, where they had to catch their flight back to Taiwan later that evening. I didn't tell them about the ice-cream mixer. The three of us sat on the bed, which made thick crinkling noises whenever one of us shifted. We didn't say very much to each other. My father seemed suddenly to have lost his energy and excitement. My mother had been quiet all afternoon, and now she held my hand, rested it on her thigh, and muttered that this bed was very bad for my back and wondered if I could trade it in for a better one.

Then my father looked at his watch and told my mother that they should get going. I slowly got up from the bed. I was surprised that I didn't want my parents to leave. Growing up, I had spent almost every summer away from home, in the States with my cousins who lived in California and New York, and one summer in England by myself. My brother was twelve and I was only nine when we took our first international flight by ourselves. The airline had allowed our father to come onto the plane until right before takeoff. We felt proud when the adult passengers watched in amazement as our father left us in our seats and walked down the narrow aisle and off the plane. We were used to saying good-bye to our parents and being on our own, and we never cried when we parted. But now, as I walked them out to the parking lot, I felt my throat closing up and pressed my lips together hard. By the car, my father hugged me first; when we pulled apart, I tried not to look into his eyes. My mother's nose was red, and she already had tears streaming down her face. When they got into the car and my father started the engine, I opened my mouth to say good-bye, but my throat burned and nothing came out. The car backed out of its space, and I looked at my parents through the windshield, their faces obscured by the reflection of the sky and overlapping leaves from a nearby tree. And then they were gone.

Until that moment, I had been confident about leaving Taiwan to live in the States. Except for two years of Taiwanese kindergarten (they run for three years from "small-" to "medium-" to "large class," like sizes of a T-shirt),

I had always gone to American school, where speaking Chinese outside of Chinese class, unless you took it as an elective, was prohibited. (Even though this rule was not strictly enforced, it was a rule, nonetheless.) The school had been established in 1949 by American GIs who were stationed on the island during the war and wanted their children to have an American education. By the time my brother and I were enrolled in the school, our classmates were mostly people like us—"American-born Chinese" (ABCs) who had returned to Taiwan; otherwise, our classmates' parents were in Taiwan on business or were teachers at our school. I had grown up not only speaking English fluently and learning about American history but also having a fairly good sense of what American culture was. Judy Blume novels and John Hughes movies gave me road maps for the complex emotions and politics of an American adolescent world. And because, during the summers, most of our parents sent us to the States, we came home in late August with all the necessary fashion trends to start the new school year—neon-colored Trapper Keepers, white Keds sneakers, braided friendship bracelets. I had only to study American pop culture closely to get my clues on how to be the American that I was within the school walls.

Outside the American school in Taipei, I was someone different. After-school snacks were unlike the pretzels, popcorn, and chocolate chip cookies that appeared on our school snack bar menu. My friends and I ate shaved ice drizzled with condensed milk in the hot summer months, grilled corn and squid on thin wooden sticks that we would buy from street vendors when it was colder. We went singing in Karaoke bars and shopping at night markets. When we were older, we would go to someone's house and play mahjong until five in the morning, snacking on squid jerky and wasabi peas and drinking from little, squat, plastic bottles of Yakult, a Japanese yogurt drink. Often, we broke out into the familiar, emphatic phrases used while playing mahjong (Pong! Chr! Hu lah!), mimicking our parents, some of whom played mahjong together on Sunday afternoons. Always while we played, we gossiped about our classmates at school and giggled girlishly over our latest crushes. Once, my father gave me a travel-size mahjong set, which I brought to school, and a group of us began playing in the cafeteria during our lunch hour. My mini mahjong set was eventually confiscated by the school; the principal was afraid we were gambling on school grounds.

Inside the American school, there was one set of rules for how to conduct oneself socially and academically. We were encouraged to be ourselves, have a personality distinct from others, speak up in class, and talk to our teachers as if they were our friends. But outside of school, there was another, entirely different set of rules for how to be—there was a different road map for Taiwanese adolescence and education. During after-school Chinese lessons, my brother and I never questioned our tutor, and we learned how to read and write Chinese characters by rote memorization. On the streets, people looked at us funny when they noticed that my brother didn't have the buzz cut and I didn't have the bowl-cut bob that were the hairstyles required by regular Chinese schools. We looked different, and that was strange.

But growing up, I had never been bothered by the physical and psychic split between in-school culture and outside-school culture. The confluence of two vastly different cultures, juxtaposed in small details like living in a small apartment off Ho-ping Road—named after two of eight Confucian virtues—while getting two days off school for Thanksgiving (during which time no one celebrated with turkey and mashed potatoes—instead, my friends and I got together for movies and more mahjong) never seemed strange to me. There was an unconscious effortlessness in accepting one culture right along with the other and fitting them both into one life. I felt I had a firm grasp of both cultures—especially American culture. When I spent time in the States during summer vacations, people often asked me where I was from, expecting me to say Queens, New Jersey, or San Francisco, depending on which coast I was visiting. There was always a moment of surprise (and pride, on my part) when I replied, "Actually, I'm from Taiwan." The summer I was ten, my parents had sent me to camp in Los Angeles, where my mother's younger sister lived.

One afternoon while I was sitting at a picnic table with a bunch of my summer friends, one girl turned to ask me if there was electricity where I was from. She had short, blond pigtails that curled in perfectly, like two C's, and thin, pink skin lightly sprinkled with freckles. Then another girl chimed in and asked if my brother and I rode the family cow to school. Maybe I was a little hurt, but it wasn't because they had failed to recognize that every toy they owned had probably been made in Taiwan—it was because I was eager to be liked, which at that age meant being just like everyone else. I didn't want to be known as the girl who read books by candlelight and woke up at daybreak to milk the cows, when, in fact, much of the technology in Taiwan was far more advanced than that in the United States. But the girls' short-lived curiosity about where I had come from was soon dispelled and forgotten, in large part because of my unaccented American English, complete with slang vocabulary; they easily accepted me to be just like them. I felt like a sly insider—one who had learned how to be American by studying CliffsNotes.

For some reason, as I watched my parents' rental car disappear down the curve of the hill and reappear again when the road straightened out at the bottom, I felt my sense of confidence begin to unravel. Perhaps it was because this was no longer just a two-month stint and I was afraid someone might expose me as an American impostor. I was not, after all, the real deal. And over the next week at school, I was surprised to find that I did not have all the information I needed to act the ideal American I thought I could be—indeed, I felt I already was. The fluidity between cultures that I had maintained when I was at home was suddenly broken. There were certain aspects about American culture, history, and humor—especially humor—that I could not understand or account for. To this day, American comedy or, say, references to The Simpsons, make me nervous because there is still that anxious desire inside me to understand, to be in on the joke, to get it. I was embarrassed for having these blank spaces in my timelines of American TV history and pop culture that, by the way people talked cavalierly, I gleaned was information everyone should know, and I was too proud to ask someone to explain. I often felt that I was at a party, talking to a group of people about something of which I knew nothing, but smiling and laughing when I was given the cues to do so but on the inside, desperately wanting to go home.

I envied the girl at Main Moon, who didn't speak English and so wasn't expected to know what people were talking about. She had a good excuse—she was an innocent outsider. And I envied Minnie Keh from across the hall because she had grown up in America and was a real insider. I decided that my father was wrong—neither of the girls could take care of me because they could never profess to understand how uncomfortable I felt knowing simultaneously too little and too much.

The easiest thing for me to do was to not ask for help or admit my loneliness but to think about how different I was from other people and how little I had in common with my classmates and everything that I was missing. Slowly, I stopped talking to people and would sometimes go through days without communicating with anyone at school, not even my roommate. I began to feel the intermittent welcome quietude and uncontainable hysteria of real, self-induced solitude. And to withdraw into myself even more, I began to think about home frequently. The image of home—tiny as though I were squinting at it through the wrong end of a telescope—became clearer and more defined than when I had lived there and had been nestled in its immediate surroundings. Yes, there was the little grocery store down the alley where my mother would send me for eggs when I was a little girl. The owner was a skinny man who wore threadbare cotton undershirts and khaki shorts that were always pulled up too high. I don't remember ever paying him cash. Instead, he would record what I had bought in a thin, square notebook on the cover of which he had carefully written the Chinese ideogram for forest—Lin. I could smell the sweetness of red bean cakes cooking on the street vendors' cast iron skillets. I could even feel the thickness of the humid summer air.

I transported myself home through that telescope of nostalgia whenever I didn't want to think about how far away from it I had traveled. But soon I discovered something that unsettled me. The more frequently I made these close examinations of home, the more frequently mao dun feelings were aroused. It wasn't so much how I felt about home that was conflicted because we all, to some extent, want to simultaneously embrace and reject home. There is something inherent in the implications of the place where we come from that makes us gravitate toward the way it defines us, all the while making us want to run as far away from its confines as possible. What unsettled me were the facts about Taiwan and the specific way that my family experienced it in relation to America, which had, until then, remained below the surface for me. With sudden clarity, I saw that the real mao dun I was feeling was the fact that even at home, I was not all that "authentic" of a Taiwanese either, having been born in the States and grown up speaking English. I ached to be entirely one way or the other when the reality was that it was not possible. And that so much of Taiwan's history was itself enmeshed in mao dun emotions was a truth that I had lived and breathed but never understood, or had ever tried to articulate.

When I was ready to try, the person I turned to was my professor for a required first-year course called "The History of Western Civilization." We had been having weekly written dialogues in which he pushed me to define "Western" and "Eastern" cultures as I experienced them. I started by positing that everything Western was all that wasn't Eastern and, in my case, that everything here, at school, was Western and everything back home in Taiwan, was Eastern. But that, of course, was a gross oversimplification of how one should define these terms, especially for someone like me, who had grown up with strong influences from both and other cultures. Then, I decided to tell him the story my father had told me about the vendor who sold the all-powerful spear alongside his indestructible shield. When I concluded, as my father had, saying mao dun was a description of an emotion, I could only come up with the English equivalent of "ambivalence." But that still seemed an inadequate translation.

Finally, I told my professor, mao dun is when your ambivalence becomes unequivocal.

Wealth Ribbon: Taiwan Bound, America Bound

LANGUAGE

1.

I do not know which language I learned to speak first. Before I became aware that the grown-ups and children around me spoke different languages, I mimicked their speech and spoke all of them with an easy, uninhibited childlike fluency—mixing and braiding languages together, conjugating verbs in one language with the rules from another. I was born into a family whose conversations at the dinner table worked like symphonies, in which the distinct tones and sounds of different instruments intertwined with each other to form a comprehensible, harmonized whole, for each generation in my family grew up speaking a different language, playing a different instrument. Sometimes the result was a cacophonous clashing of unidentifiable utterances. Sometimes we did not understand each other at all and silence would replace our inability to communicate. Perhaps most often, not speaking became the way we truly understood one another—this silent language becoming the one tongue that we all spoke with astounding fluency. But before I was old enough to unbraid the strands of languages that I knew from my everyday life, I claimed all of them as one.

For the first four years of my life, I lived with my mother and brother in a house in San Francisco. I don't remember much about the interior of the house, but I can picture the backyard with such precise detail that I am sure I have architectured this exactitude to make up for the vagueness and fragmentation of my other memories from that time. There was a tree in the center of our yard around the base of which someone had built a circular wooden bench. When I sat on the bench and let my head roll back and my mouth fall open, I remember that I saw no sky—only little holes of light shifting playfully between the gaps in the leaves. My brother, Alex, who was three years older and already in school, often brought his friends, Gregory and Cliff, to our house after school. The three of them would yank our red tent from the closet and drag it out into the yard. They pitched the tent and ducked inside, one after another. The last one zipped up the entrance with a zzzzt that sealed the dome with finality, leaving me alone outside. They stayed in the tent until sundown. By dusk, all I could see was the soft yellow glow of a flashlight jumping back and forth as the boys jerked it out of one another's hands to shine on what I can only guess were Marvel comic books. The light seemed to hum with luminescence from the inner cavity of the tent—a forbidden and secret world to which I was not invited. The lone bulb created a soft orange halo around the tent with the gauzy texture of smudged colored chalk.

Though my brother couldn't stand having me anywhere near him and his friends (he believed I was superfluous to the family and felt a natural resentment toward me with the self-centeredness of a six-year-old), I managed to stand as close to—and as far away from—them as possible so that I could listen hard for the secrets they were exchanging. They used English words like funny, Spiderman, and give it back! There are pictures of me standing there, outside the tent with my balled-up fists sitting insistently on my hips—obviously, my mother or an aunt or uncle found my exclusion from my brother's world humorous. On my own, I repeated the words silently and checked them with my brother whenever I could. I found I could "converse" with him best on Saturday mornings when he sat with his face practically pressed against the television to watch cartoons. Images of Wile E. Coyote with scribbled, whirlpool-like legs chasing the blank-faced Road Runner so captured my brother's attention that I believe he hardly noticed my presence. Whenever he laughed, I took my cue and shouted, "Funny!" Absently, he answered by laughing harder and maybe once or twice, he turned his head slightly to look my way. Unknowingly, my brother taught me my first English words.

We were living in San Francisco in the late 1970s, waiting for my mother to become an American citizen. My father worked for Texas Instruments in Taiwan and was able to get his citizenship that way. We were to move back to Taiwan to join him as soon as my mother got her passport.

Making each of us an American citizen was my parents' "fall-back plan" in case Communist China decided to invade and take over Taiwan.

During our four years in San Francisco, my mother worked at a lab downtown. Every morning after she dropped my brother off at school, my mother would take me to my babysitter's house and then go to work. Mrs. Fan—Fan Tai Tai—had come from Hong Kong and spoke Cantonese. She spoke limited Mandarin—guo yu, national language—the official spoken and written Chinese taught in schools on Mainland China and Taiwan. Every Chinese province also has its own distinct dialect, which is a loose derivative of Mandarin. The language breaks down even further between cities and towns within a province—dialects that are derivatives of a derivative. At home, my mother spoke a mixture of Mandarin and Taiwanese to us.

Fan Tai Tai had a grandson, Eddie, whom she took care of while babysitting me. He was a year or two older than I, chubby, and always had a smile that would sink back into his double chin as his little black eyes narrowed sleepily, contentedly. He reminded me of the Cheshire Cat—his smiles seemed to place him in another world, and I often felt he might slowly become transparent and then disappear altogether, leaving just his thin, curved lips.

Eddie and I would run around Fan Tai Tai's house, chasing each other as she prepared lunch in the kitchen. We padded down the dim hallways and in and out of even dimmer rooms. The smells of fried fish and ginger wafted through the house. When we slowed down our running, panting as we slumped onto the living room couch, Eddie would crane his neck to look at his grandmother cooking in the kitchen and report back to me with an expectant grin. Lunch was ready. The three of us sat around Fan Tai Tai's small kitchen table, plates of food steaming before us. While Eddie picked up his bowl and frantically shoveled rice and vegetables into his mouth with his chopsticks, Fan Tai Tai would place little mounds of rice at the bottom of a ceramic spoon and top it with morsels of fish, carefully plucking out invisible bones with her wrinkled fingers, and put each spoonful lovingly into my opened, eager mouth.

My mother has told me that during the time Fan Tai Tai was my babysitter, I had been fluent in Cantonese. This never ceases to surprise and delight me because I have long since forgotten how to speak the dialect. That I was once fluent in a tongue I can no longer speak makes me think I might have been an entirely different person then. I would not be able to converse with that person now. A few years ago, while visiting my grandparents in San Francisco, my mother suddenly came up with the idea to drive over to Fan Tai Tai's house to say hello. It had been almost fifteen years since I'd seen my babysitter. I asked my mother if she had been keeping in touch with Fan Tai Tai, and she said she had, but only erratically. I thought I remembered seeing pictures of Eddie and his older sisters at the zoo in some random drawer at home. He was maybe thirteen or fourteen years old, wearing a blue polo shirt, and was tanned. The sun had been strong that day, and Eddie had squinted into the camera. His cheeks had still been round with preadolescent pudginess.

"Do you know if they're going to be home?" I asked my mother, suddenly getting nervous that they might be. What would I say to them? What language would I speak?

My mother didn't seem to hear my question; she had a faraway smile on her face. Driving down those familiar streets must have transported her back to a different time—a time when she and my father only saw each other once every two to three months, a time when she was still young and things were tough and she was probably often lonely, but it was a time that she could now look back upon with bittersweet nostalgia. "We're here!" she said suddenly, breaking her own reverie. We had pulled up along the curb across from Fan Tai Tai's house. I don't think I had ever known what the outside of the house looked like, and though it was only a few years ago that my mother and I sat in the car with the ignition still running across from Fan Tai Tai's house, I still cannot recall the shape, size, or color of the house. But I knew exactly what the house would smell like once Fan Tai Tai opened the front door.

My mother and I sat in the car for a while, both of us peering at the house through the car window—she with girl-like excitement, I with mounting unease. "It looks dark in there," my mother considered. "Could they have gone out?" Her hand clutched the door handle and pulled. The car door popped open. "You wait here," she said. "I'll go look." I watched as my mother crossed the street and walked up to the front door. She knocked on the door and waited. She looked back at me and shrugged her shoulders. She walked out onto the front lawn and tiptoed to reach the window, cupping her hands around her eyes to peer into the house. I prayed that no one was home. I could already see us sitting in the living room with glasses of cold barley tea sweating in our hands. Fan Tai Tai would smile at me, and I would smile back, not knowing what to say. How strange that I would not be able to tell the person who had taken care of me the first four years of my life anything much more than, "I'm fine." I felt an embarrassment for having unlearned my babysitter's language; in a sense, I felt as though, by losing our linguistic connection, I had undone our once-intimate and familiar relationship. Finally, and to my guilty relief, my mother turned from the window and shrugged her shoulders at me again, walking back to the car.

When we lived in San Francisco, we had spent a lot of time with my mother's parents, who lived just twenty minutes away from us in a baby-blue house on a hill overlooking Golden Gate Park. My grandmother had grown up during the Japanese occupation of Taiwan and had been sent to Japan for medical school. She had become one of the first female ophthalmologists in Taiwan and practiced in Taichung—a city southwest of the capital—for more than forty years before she and my grandfather had retired to San Francisco. There, my grandmother filled her days with cooking—something she loved to do but rarely had time for when she was an eye doctor. My mother told me that the nurses usually prepared lunch and dinner and the only time my grandmother had a chance to cook for the family was during the week-long Chinese New Year break. In San Francisco, my grandmother took the bus down the hill to shop in the Chinese markets along Clement Street. Over time, she became friends with the bus drivers; the fishmongers; and the man who sold her glistening, roasted ducks that hung upside down in his shop window. Every year, for Chinese New Year, she would give each of them a slightly-perfumed red envelope with crisp tens and twenties tucked inside. My grandmother pickled her own vegetables and fruits, filling large mason jars with plums, and seeping them in brandy. She kept these jars in the garage, where it was dark and cool. She put the vegetables and plums on little plates when she had company and served them as snacks, giving whole jars away as gifts.

After my grandfather graduated from art school, he did not paint for a long while. Instead, he fell in and out of odd jobs—working in pharmaceuticals and writing articles for the local Taichung newspapers—and formed an art society called "Move" with friends who liked to get together to discuss art over Chinese tea. He didn't paint again until he was sixty years old and had moved to America. He had always admired the freedom, independence, and creativity of the American spirit, and I think he needed to marry that energy with the discipline of his traditional Confucian background to rediscover his inspiration to paint. In San Francisco, he went to the art academy downtown almost every day to paint from live models—he maintained this routine even toward the end of his life, when he would sometimes lose his way home. I often wondered what the other art students, most of whom were in their twenties, thought of my grandfather. I wondered if he made conversation with them, taking out his mini English-Chinese dictionary from his shirt pocket whenever someone said a word he did not understand. I wondered whether the other students thought my grandfather was a good artist.

After my grandfather died, my grandmother found a pencil drawing that someone from my grandfather's class had made of him. In the portrait, my grandfather was wearing a knitted cap, one of his many plaid shirts, suspenders, and a pair of his corduroy pants. He was sitting in a chair, his arms folded across his large stomach. His big, round glasses had slipped down his nose. He had fallen asleep in class—his chin resting easily on his chest—as he often did unconsciously at the dinner table in the last few years of his life. Every time this happened, my mother would kick me under the table as though we were two young girls in class while her face betrayed an expression of sadness and uncompromising love for her father.

My grandfather kept a "studio" in the basement of the house, where he stored his paintings and art books but never worked. He was a private painter, rarely sharing his work with his family. I have no idea what my grandfather looked like when he was painting—even in his classmate's drawing of him, he was in repose, but I can imagine his inner passion, which he unabashedly expressed on the canvas.

When one particular painting was nearly finished, my grandfather would bring it home from the academy and set it on the floor next to the mantel in the living room. Every day, he walked by the painting, squinted his eyes at it, walked up close, and studied it. Meanwhile, my grandmother stood behind him, watching him but not saying a word. A few days later, the painting would go back to the art academy with my grandfather, where he would make the necessary changes and sign his name on the bottom right-hand corner— Y. T. Lan—the letters tilting upward as if on the incline of a hill.

Sometimes my grandmother would bring lunch to my grandfather at the art school, and while she waited for him in the hallway, she would rummage in the trash cans and salvage drawings and paintings that my grandfather had thrown away. She smoothed them out gently and took them home, framing the ones she liked. Once, she made a gift of one of them—a small study executed quickly on scrap paper of a young girl's profile resting on the back of her bent arm—for my parents. She told them that something about the girl's concentrated, yet languid, look reminded her of me.

My grandparents—I called them Taichung Ah-gong and Taichung Ah-ma—were very different people. When I was older, I noticed that they barely spoke the same language, Taichung Ah-ma's most fluent language being Japanese, and Taichung Ah-gong's a hybrid of Mandarin, Taiwanese, some Japanese, and Hakka—a Chinese dialect belonging to a small tribe of Han Chinese who, long ago, had kept migrating southward until they reached Taiwan to avoid internecine wars on the mainland. In fact, my grandparents shared a secret, almost nonverbal language that they had developed through their more than sixty years of marriage. Although their personalities seemed as distinct as I could imagine two people to have, together they made sense. One always seemed to be able to anticipate what the other needed; their movements dovetailed effortlessly into one fluid motion. They admired each other with the same freshness and naiveté as when they had first met when my grandfather was a reporter and had heard about a beautiful lady eye doctor in Taichung and asked the paper if he could do a story on her.

From Taichung Ah-gong and Taichung Ah-ma, I learned bits and pieces of all the different languages they spoke. I imagine that when I was young, I must have mixed them all together and concocted my own version of their language. What resulted was a verbal representation of the way they communicated without words: disparate parts culled together to make a coherent, sensible whole. I feel I must have been a part of my grandparents' private world of communicative gestures and emotions that transcended linguistic boundaries—this world made all the more private by their limited English; besides each other and family, with whom did my grandparents converse? In what language?

The older I got, the more fluent I became in English and Mandarin, while my comprehension of the other languages faded. They were not wholly unfamiliar—I could speak and understand Taiwanese, but only haltingly and without the boldness of a child uninhibited by self-consciousness. And I still carried particular vocabulary words from Japanese and Hakka around in my head, though I could no longer understand complete sentences. I remember very little from all those visits to my grandparents' house in San Francisco during our four years living there. But when I think of that time, I miss my grandparents with a very specific pang for which I do not know the name. Even though I have visited with them many more times after my family moved back to Taiwan, I have never been able to regain the fluency with which I could converse with them when I was a young child.

The only real visual memory I have of being at my grandparents' house during those four years in San Francisco is of Taichung Ah-gong washing his face in the pink-tiled bathroom before going to bed. I remember this because it was a ritual for me to watch him every time I spent the night. He would be wearing one of his thin, white undershirts, his belly protruding and stretching the material taut. When I stood next to him, my eyes were level to his round stomach. He did everything slowly and carefully, wringing out his hot facecloth many times before he pressed it into his face, creating a cloud of steam around his face. Then, he pushed three fingers gently into each eye socket. And finally, I would hear him sigh with satisfaction into the cloth. When he was finished, he would take another facecloth, wet it, wring it, and bring it to my face. He held the back of my head with one hand while the other one rubbed my face with the washcloth in a circular motion. As he did this, he sang, "Sui ah, sui ah"—"Beauty, oh, beauty!" in Taiwanese. It was as if he were rubbing beauty right into my face. And when he finished, he helped hoist me up so that I could support myself on the sink with my elbows and look at myself in the steamy mirror. My cheeks would be rosy, my eyelashes wet, and my eyes bright. It was Taichung Ah-gong who had given me my Chinese name: Po (pine tree) wei (wild rose).

2.

The person in my family with whom I most identified this feeling of being simultaneously fluent in many languages and not fluent in any at all was my father's mother, my other ah-ma. Like Taichung Ah-ma, she had studied medicine in Japan and after she graduated, became one of the first female pediatricians in Taipei. She spoke Japanese, Mandarin, Taiwanese, and English. She could even speak a little German, which I found out when I temporarily lived in a house my grandmother owned in San Francisco right after I finished college and discovered that the shelves in her living room were stacked with thick, brown volumes of medical journals, all of them in German. My grandmother spoke all of these languages but was always complaining that she couldn't speak any of them well enough.

My cousin Gary once told me this story about talking with our grandmother: One day, Gary called her on the phone and immediately started to converse with her in Taiwanese, knowing that she could understand Taiwanese better than she could English. He, like all my other cousins on my father's side, had grown up in the States and didn't speak much Mandarin. His parents had taught him and his sisters to speak Taiwanese at home, and he could understand the dialect well, though he spoke it with a thick American accent. He had just begun college and started to tell our grandmother how things were going when she stopped him short and said impatiently, "Please. Speak English to me. I don't understand a word you're saying!" When Gary told me this, he laughed humbly about his sorry version of Taiwanese. I thought about it later and realized that my grandmother had never asked me to speak or not speak a particular language with her. I always spoke with her in a mix of Mandarin, Taiwanese, and English, as she did with me. It was what came naturally for both of us. We could complete thoughts much more adequately when we allowed each other to substitute a Chinese word with a better English one, and vice versa. What Gary's story showed was not how terrible his Taiwanese was but how much easier my grandmother could communicate by speaking a hybrid of different languages. I wondered whether it was also in this multicultural tongue that she had her most private thoughts or dreamed.

One of the first things I had heard about my grandmother was that she had gone on an African safari all by herself when she was young. No one actually told me this piece of information; I gathered it myself by listening to the adults' conversations. I would move from adult to adult, my head level with their elbows propped up against the table, hands cupping little brown ceramic teacups. Sometimes someone—usually my mother—would absently put her hand on my head, acknowledging me but not really aware that I was listening.

I remember thinking my grandmother's trip to Africa the most original thing a grandmother could do. But for my grandmother, it wasn't so extraordinary because she was always traveling, always going somewhere with friends or by herself. I could easily picture her in my mind, standing by a jeep with one hand gently touching the car door and the other reaching up toward the curling, smiling trunk of an elephant with thin, flapping ears the shape of Africa. She wore a khaki shirt with the first few buttons undone and a brightly colored scarf tied carelessly around her neck, the knot shooting out into two little rabbit ears. Her silver hair blew in her face—bronzed by the sun—some of the hair caught in her open, laughing mouth. The wind around her kicked up dust. Even though no one had ever told me that she could speak an African language, I assumed my grandmother could.

I started to call her "Africa Ah-ma," which made her laugh and rub my head and call me ah gao, "little pet" in Taiwanese. This only confirmed everything I imagined about her African safari. Her identity—her nationality—seemed to have an effortless fluidity to it. I could place her in any one of the places she'd been to, and the fluency with which she spoke a certain language and adapted a certain culture was a thing I could—and would—easily assume. The notion of an international and global identity seems a rather recent one—one that belongs to my generation. Certainly, when my grandmother was young in the 1930s and 1940s, nationality was a much more rigid idea in which geographical boundaries drew stark lines that differentiated between cultures, ethnicities, languages, and allegiances. But my ah-ma seemed to embody a global identity and world view well beyond her time. The pastiche of languages that this grandmother spoke differed from the one my Taichung grandparents spoke because she was less shy and reserved. Hers was a language I could hear, rather than one I felt or saw described by quiet gestures and expressions.

When the syllables in "Africa Ah-ma" began to trip my tongue, I decided I needed to come up with another name for her. The other place I associated her with was America, Meiguo—"beautiful country." In the 1970s, "Meiguo Ah-ma" had moved to California with all her children (except my father, who stayed in Taiwan) and bought a one-bedroom condominium in San Mateo that had a pool and Jacuzzi on the first floor. When she came to visit us in Taiwan, at least one of her suitcases would be stuffed with colorful boxes of cereal for my brother and me. Wedged tightly between the cereal boxes were T-shirts and sweatshirts from the different places she'd visited. She was an expert packer from being such an experienced traveler. When she came to Taiwan, Meiguo Ah-ma was usually en route to somewhere else. In my mind, she was the quintessential independent American woman who was single and strong, a product of the Feminist movement who seemingly didn't need anyone. On one of her visits when I was still in kindergarten, I remember asking her how long she planned to stay. It was early afternoon, and we were the only ones at home. We sat in the middle of the living room couch as the afternoon sun slanted in from the balcony window, slicing the living room in half. Ah-ma shot a look of disapproval at me, her eyes angry and, I thought, a little hurt.

"What—you want Ah-ma to leave already?"

Frightened, I whimpered, "no."

"Because I can, you know," she said, looking away. "There are lots of places I can go."

Meiguo Ah-ma intimidated me because she was on guard and seemed always ready to push people away, but I mostly admired her—not for that particular quality, but for the reason she had become the way she was. She had lived through two world wars, and her husband had died when he was just forty years old, leaving her to raise five children on her own. No one could go through a life like hers and not develop a certain hardness. Meiguo Ah-ma's occasional brusqueness was something we knew she had, in a sense, earned, and so we overlooked it. My other grandmother, Taichung Ah-ma, was strong in a different way—she was my grandfather's wife, one part of a pair inextricably tied to the other.

When I look through old sepia photographs of my grandmothers when they were young, I am always surprised at how much the expressions in their faces reveal about their personalities. Taichung Ah-ma smiled with her lips closed, the corners curling up just a little. She had thin, dramatically-arched eyebrows and soft curls that framed her round face. She was known around Taichung for her beauty—a mysterious, quiet beauty that was a gentle blend of Japanese modesty and Taiwanese naiveté. Meiguo Ah-ma, on the other hand, smiled in all her photographs with her teeth showing, her eyes flirting with the camera and one hip lower than the other in a carefree stance. She was beautiful because of the openness in her face. There was a light in her eyes that invited you to share her excitement for life, her curiosity for everything new. Her clothes were modern, too. I remember loving how Western she looked in her short dresses, fancy hats, and big movie-star sunglasses. She even managed to put a twist on the traditional high-collared qi pao that Chinese women wear on special occasions. One of hers was a black, slim dress that she had tailor-made—black lace layered atop a silk chemise that revealed just the smallest area of bare skin above her chest. In these photographs, all the other women look stiff and bound by their qi pao; Meiguo Ah-ma looks radiant, playful.

The story of how Meiguo Ah-ma acquired knowledge of so many different languages is inextricably tied to the political story of Taiwan from 1895 until after World War II.

In 1895, after China lost the first Sino-Japanese war, Taiwan was ceded to Japan "in perpetuity." When the Japanese landed on the island in 1895, they were met with passionate resistance. The Taiwanese, angered by the mainland's abandonment and unwilling to be colonized by their recent enemy, declared independence by establishing the Republic of Taiwan on May 25 that same year. Probably very few people know that Taiwan was the first Asian republic; it lasted for a mere ten days. Still, "the Republic of

Taiwan" resounds in my ears like a full-bodied gong, reverberating through my body, sending up a surge of pride. But at the end of this rumble, when the vibrations have slowed down and the pitch softens and evaporates into the air, I feel sadness for the almost immediately shattered hope of a people's determination to govern itself. The Taiwanese fought Japanese troops for four months before surrendering the southern port city of Tainan. Resistance against colonization continued sporadically throughout the island—some say for twenty years—and an estimated 10,000 Taiwanese were killed in the process. The island was officially surrendered and forced under Japanese occupation by October 1895 and would remain so for the next fifty years.

The Japanese instituted many reforms: They restricted the use of opium, which the British had introduced to China in exchange for tea and spices; cut off the long, single braids that men were accustomed to wearing; and banned the traditional practice of binding women's feet—both of these being symbols of dynastic Chinese rule. Meiguo Ah-ma's mother was only too happy to comply with the last reform, relieved that her two daughters wouldn't have to suffer the excruciating pain of bones cracking and splitting when the toes were curled under and tightly bound, as hers were, to form the perfect pair of "three-inch lotus feet." The Japanese rewarded those who accepted their reforms with positions as teachers in the new education system and sometimes even offered them jobs as officials in the new colonial administration. By including and co-opting the Taiwanese into their system, the Japanese were able to successfully introduce new technology, agriculture, economic freedom, and bureaucratic efficiency to the island.

When Meiguo Ah-ma was born in 1915, the island had already been occupied by the Japanese for twenty years and had seen that Japanese rule had brought about many positive changes. Trade increased, agriculture progressed, infrastructure was developed, per capita income rose, and the quality of people's lives was improving at a rate that the mainland, whose last dynasty had fallen in 1912, could not possibly match. This was one of the many inherent mao duns of colonization: On the one hand, Taiwan would have preferred that its republic had lasted longer than those pathetic ten days; on the other hand, the island could not deny that its social and economic progress was owed mostly to Japanese rule.

Meiguo Ah-ma grew up going to Japanese schools in Taipei. At school, she spoke Japanese, and at home with her parents, she spoke Taiwanese. People of my grandmother's generation were given the opportunity to pursue a professional Japanese education (usually medicine) that would ensure their future wealth and prestige. When she graduated at the top of her high school class, Meiguo Ah-ma's mother wanted to send her to a Japanese medical school in Tokyo even though my grandmother had very different plans for her own future.

Meiguo Ah-ma wanted to be a dressmaker. She wanted to learn how to make the gorgeous kimonos that she saw her Japanese classmates and her classmates' mothers wear in Taipei. The fabric—usually raw silk—from which kimonos were made rustled and whispered as the wearer walked in small steps down the streets. The outfit lent such an air of mystery and elegance to the woman wearing it that my grandmother wanted to understand its mystery from the inside out. Doubtless, once she learned how to make a traditional kimono, Meiguo Ah-ma would have taken it further and designed kimonos with her own unique and more modern variations.

But my grandmother never became a kimono designer. Meiguo Ah-ma's parents were adamant that she take the opportunity the Japanese government was giving to able Taiwanese to pursue a professional Japanese education. Reluctantly, Meiguo Ah-ma enrolled in medical school in Tokyo. Meanwhile, in Taipei, Meiguo Ah-ma's mother began the second part of her plan for her daughter's future. She began arranging a marriage.

A family friend had a son who was also going to medical school in Japan. The families got along well, the son had a promising future, and the families agreed that the two young medical students made a perfect match because they shared such similar backgrounds: They were both from Taiwanese families who had assimilated, in public ways, seamlessly into the Japanese culture and way of life, while at home, in private, they still spoke Taiwanese with one another and held onto their own cultural roots and traditions. There is a Chinese saying that if the doors of the bride and groom's houses are upright and their households match, the marriage would be a good one. The families in Taipei met for dinner and clinked teacups across the round table to congratulate each other on the marriage arrangement.

They sent letters to their children in Tokyo and told them the news.

Before my grandmother had met her future husband, she had decided she would hate him. It was embarrassing to a woman as independent and free-spirited as my grandmother to have to suffer the banality of such a cliché—an arranged marriage. But to defy her parents was an alternative she dared not entertain. There was too much weight in what her parents had given her to deny her family this marriage. Filial piety—unbounded obedience and duty to one's parents—was one of the five Confucian virtues that one should never abandon. Indignantly, Meiguo Ah-ma decided that the only way she could "win" in this unjust transaction was by remaining cool and impenetrable to this future husband. Then she could hold onto a part of her that would always remain hers.

Whenever this young man was instructed by parents and grandparents from both families to take my grandmother out on weekends, he showed up at her dormitory promptly, sometimes with a small gift and always with a good-natured smile and attitude. He had round cheeks, a high forehead, and full lips—all traits that "face readers" (like fortune tellers and palm readers) regard as signs of good character. To appease her family, my grandmother obligingly went on these dates. And despite the intelligence, sense of humor, and kindheartedness the young man displayed through their conversations, Meiguo Ah-ma continued to show him how she hated the idea of being forced to marry him.

Just how cruel and cold my grandmother was to my grandfather I will never know, she will probably never tell, and I know never to ask. I didn't even know my grandparents' marriage had been arranged until I was nineteen and, while on a family reunion in Florida, Meiguo Ah-ma and I shared a hotel room, she told me this story before we went to bed one night. My grandfather had already been dead for twenty-some years by the time I was born; he was barely more than a portrait on the wall of my father's study. Even though every year, on December 28th, my family commemorated his death, his memorial had always been overshadowed by the excitement of family winter vacations in tropical places. Except for on December 28th, Meiguo Ah-ma seldom talked about her husband. I know I must have thought about what my grandparents were like together as a couple, but I was still surprised when

Meiguo Ah-ma told me that, over time, she and my grandfather fell deeply in love with one another in spite of the circumstances of their marriage. That my grandmother took out her bitterness on my grandfather for a brief period of time became the one thing she regretted in her life. Had she known earlier that he was the truly wonderful man he was and that she would come to love him and he would love her, too—had she known he would die so young, leaving her and their five children, she would have acted differently.

After my grandfather died, there were many suitors; my grandmother was still an attractive, young, and successful woman. She paid none of them any attention and instead became resentful of the doctors who had brought her husband home the night he died. He had been at a dinner party and complained of feeling ill. His doctor friends brought him home and left him on the couch with my grandmother hovering over him, wiping his forehead with a damp, warm towel, and an hour later, my grandfather had died. Meiguo Ah-ma became disillusioned with the community that she and her husband were a part of and one day left her five children with the nanny and traveled around the world. This was the "African safari" everyone says my grandmother had gone on. Suddenly, my grandmother being this independent woman who traveled the whole world took on a different meaning—suddenly, she became an independent woman who traveled the world to escape. And her independence—her insistence in remaining single and loyal to her dead husband after forty years—was this, in part, her self-imposed punishment for having treated him badly when they first met?

My grandmother and I were lying in bed with the sterile-smelling hotel sheets pulled tightly across our chests. When she spoke of her regret, I felt as though an immeasurable space separated us. She spoke with a pain that I could not touch and could not profess to understand.

Before my grandfather died, he and my grandmother were both prominent doctors in Taipei. Meiguo Ah-ma was a pediatrician, and her husband was the director of the ear, nose, and throat department at the National Taiwan University Hospital. Under the Japanese occupation, they were a part of the new elite Taiwanese class who had been encouraged by the Japanese to make the best of their colonization. Because people like my grandparents owed their position in Taiwanese society to the Japanese, they developed an identity closely linked to the Japanese and their culture. They had many Japanese friends; spoke fluent Japanese in public, Taiwanese with each other at home; and hardly knew how to speak any Mandarin, which was the official national language in mainland China.

But underlying all the ways in which Taiwan benefited from Japanese rule remained the fact that Japan was Taiwan's colonizer and that the Japanese still considered themselves superior to the Taiwanese. The Taiwanese were deeply ambivalent about whether to align themselves with their Japanese colonizers or with the Chinese on the mainland, the ancestral homeland for most islanders. When Japan went to war with China for the second time in 1937, news of the Rape of Nanking—where 370,000 Chinese civilians were slaughtered; 80,000 women and girls were raped, mutilated, and murdered; and others were used for inhumane experiments—was carefully and deliberately kept from the Taiwanese. The Rape of Nanking was an atrocity my grandmother did not learn about until after Japan had withdrawn its rule over Taiwan at the end of World War II. When she told me this, Meiguo Ah-ma's face had been stricken with a look of hurt and anger. Even so many years after the fact, I could tell that at times she was still unable to fully reconcile the part of her identity that is Japanese with the part that is Chinese and Taiwanese. She was, by indirect association, simultaneously the perpetrator of the crime and the victim. I can only imagine the feelings of horror, betrayal, and even guilt that she felt when she finally did learn about what happened at the Rape of Nanking.

When Japan lost the war in 1945, it withdrew its government from Taiwan. The island was once again in limbo, but only briefly, as it had been for ten days in 1895. In a meeting between President Roosevelt, Prime Minister Churchill, and Generalissimo Chiang Kai-shek, who was the self-proclaimed leader of the Republic of China, it was agreed that Taiwan should be restored to the Republic of China as a province. Despite Taiwan's technological, educational, and social advancements as a result of the Japanese occupation, they still resented their colonial status so that when the island was returned to the mainland, their ambivalence about their national and cultural identity quickly gave way to euphoria: Most Taiwanese considered mainland China the homeland of their culture and ancestors. They expected Chiang Kai-shek's Chinese Nationalists (the Kuomintang, or KMT) to be the liberators from fifty years of Japanese occupation. And likewise, the Nationalists expected to be readily embraced by the Taiwanese because they felt the Taiwanese had been tainted by Japanese culture and deprived of Chinese culture for too long. But no one was prepared for what the Restoration would, in fact, bring to Taiwan's future.

When Taiwan was restored to the Republic of China, it was done so to a China on shaky ground. The end of World War II did not coincide with the end of fighting in China; Mao Zedong's Communist and Chiang Kai-shek's Nationalist united front against the Japanese broke up again, and the civil war continued and intensified. Mao's army had a strong hold on northern China while Chiang ruled in the south. After the Japanese withdrew from Taiwan, Chiang appointed a man named Chen Yi to be governor of Taiwan. One of the first things that Chen Yi did when he arrived in Taiwan was require everyone to learn to speak Mandarin. He vehemently believed that a common language would unify the country, and he would not tolerate anyone speaking any other dialect of Chinese. He refused to speak Japanese, even though he had been educated in Japan and spoke the language fluently, and had to have been aware that his Japanese would have helped him communicate with the many Taiwanese like my grandparents who spoke better Japanese than they did Mandarin. Governor Chen Yi appointed all new officials to his cabinet and disappointed the many Taiwanese who, under the Japanese, had held high government positions because not one of them was appointed. As a result, about 36,000 Taiwanese officials lost their jobs. Stripped of economic and political stability, many Taiwanese started to resent the new Nationalist government and became suspicious of its intentions.

Much of what I know about Taiwan's history, I know from reading books published in English or books written in Chinese that have been translated into English. My spoken Chinese is far superior to my written Chinese, and as a result, I cannot read in Chinese as swiftly or as comprehensively as I can in English. But English books on Taiwan are limited, and the books that do exist are often dry and unimaginative. Mere facts and timelines are hardly adequate to reveal the deep and hidden emotional struggles that make a nation and a people what and who they are. History's great moments—triumphs, failures, atrocities, and achievements—are enmeshed in the mundane routine of which we are all a part; it is the ordinary that makes the extraordinary transcendent. It requires a lot of imagination to understand our past, ourselves. I struggled with the books I read about Taiwan's past because the events that were described felt so removed from me, almost foreign, just words crawling across a page. In high school, we were required to take one semester of East Asian history, but then, as was the case with most teenagers, I cared very little about the past and little about the future, luxuriating in the exciting, day-to-day melodramas of the youthful present.

Now, I wanted to be connected to the past, and I knew I needed someone to be my liaison. Two years ago, Meiguo Ah-ma came to New York in October to stay with my aunt in Queens for a few days. It was then that I decided my grandmother would be the one to help me make that leap in my imagination.

It was a cold, wet morning in New York the day I went for my interview with Meiguo Ah-ma in Forest Hills. In my bag, I carried a list of questions, a tape recorder, a pen, and my notebook. I stopped for a minute before I rang the doorbell of the small, white house my aunt's family has lived in for thirty years. She had moved to New York after also graduating from a medical school in Japan. I was nervous—and embarrassed at being nervous—fearing that my grandmother might not want to do the interview anymore. When I had called her and told her that I would like to ask her some questions—and that was exactly how vaguely I'd put it—she had seemed hesitant at first but then quickly agreed to an interview without asking me what it was for. I rang the doorbell and heard my grandmother shuffle toward the door as she said something to my aunt with her head turned away from the door.

Meiguo Ah-ma opened the door. She was wearing a bright pink shirt and had a black cashmere shawl wrapped around her narrow, sloping shoulders. We paused for a moment, looking at each other. Her head wobbled on her thin neck from left to right, her left hand was hidden behind the door, and her right hand was tentatively raised as though she had forgotten why she had raised it at all. Then she pulled me into the house and asked me three times whether I had really eaten breakfast already, looking at me suspiciously each time I told her I had. She sat me down at the dining table, went into the kitchen, made me coffee, and brought out a few slices of peaches. She was about to cut a slice of coffee cake for herself when I gently admonished her, telling her she should watch her sugar intake because of her diabetes, and she mock-glared at me, muttering that I should learn to be less bossy. But I could see that my bossiness pleased her—it made her feel taken care of.

It had been about half a year since I had last seen my grandmother, but always when we see each other, it feels as though no time has elapsed. Likewise, when I call her on the telephone—something I do rarely and usually only on a whim—she talks as if continuing a conversation from yesterday. I took out my notebook, questions, and tape recorder. She acted as though she had not seen me do this and got a small, candlelight-shaped light bulb from a closet and asked me to change one of the broken light bulbs in the chandelier over the dining table. There were a few stray pieces of elongated, diamond-shaped glass from the chandelier on the table. Meiguo Ah-ma was in the midst of shining these with a dirtied, white handkerchief.

"I made this chandelier myself, you know," she said to me in Taiwanese. "Thirty-some years ago." I was standing awkwardly with one leg on the dining table and the other leg planted on a nearby chair for balance. I twisted the new light bulb into the chandelier, and the hanging glass pieces tinkled like wind chimes. I looked down and saw my grandmother smiling up at me through the glass prisms and felt her hand reach over to hold my leg.

"I didn't know that, Ah-ma," I said and held the glass pieces in my hands and admired her work. Then I came down from the table and sat down in my chair, touching my notebook gingerly. Finally, my grandmother sat down next to me, and we looked at each other awkwardly as I pushed the record button with a loud click.

I began by asking her a few basic questions—her memories about the end of the war, what she had felt when she heard that Taiwan would be restored to the Republic of China, what she thought of Chiang Kai-shek's government. She answered slowly at first, having to take time to think. But soon, she stopped listening to my questions—she did not need them anymore to prompt her memories. Her gray eyes looked to a place I could at first only imagine. And then, just as I started to hear the immediacy of the emotions in her voice, I was transported back in time with her. I saw a Taiwan that was a different place, a place seemingly worlds apart from the Taiwan where I had grown up. As my grandmother spoke, my imagination quickly filled in the details that she had forgotten. We were there together.

After Restoration, Taiwan became very confused. Nothing was restored to the Taiwanese. In fact, the order that had been a part of their daily lives under Japanese occupation was quickly disassembled. Meiguo Ah-ma and all her friends had actually gotten along quite well with the Japanese soldiers. Those soldiers had been clean-shaven, their uniforms always pressed. When they were invited inside for a cup of tea, the Japanese soldiers knew to unlace their boots before entering someone's house. My grandmother and her friends even sang folk songs about how much they liked these Japanese soldiers. She sang a snippet from the song to me, and though I have replayed this section of the tape numerous times, I can still barely make out the lyrics. But the shaky, high tone of my grandmother's singing, vibrating like the quiet beginnings of a teakettle's whistle, is clear.

When the KMT soldiers came to the island, Meiguo Ah-ma and her friends laughed aloud when they saw the pitiful, dirty, and disorganized soldiers from the mainland. The Japanese soldiers had always stood upright and carried their rifles across their backs. The Chinese soldiers' uniforms were tattered, and instead of rifles, they carried torn umbrellas and dirty bundles of blankets on their backs.

Then there was a rumor that these soldiers were extremely poor and had gone through many hardships to get to Taiwan. One person even claimed the soldiers had had to walk all the way from inland China to the coast, where they could board a ship to come to Taiwan. When Meiguo Ah-ma heard this, she felt sorry for these soldiers and sorrier still that she had laughed at them. She and some nurses carried a few tables out to the street in front of the clinic and prepared tea and snacks for any KMT soldier they saw walking by. Sometimes she would invite soldiers inside the clinic and offer them a seat.

She didn't like the fact that not one of these soldiers ever bothered to take off his dirty shoes before entering the clinic, but she wouldn't say anything. It was so hard, the long journey these soldiers had had to take!

When these soldiers did come into the clinic, Meiguo Ah-ma had difficulty communicating with them. She was in her late twenties and was just learning how to speak Mandarin because the new Nationalist government required it. Many times, when these soldiers discovered that she could not speak Mandarin fluently, they would be impatient and short with her. They called her stupid, and ri ben gui zi—"Japanese ghost." Fluency in the same language that had so recently helped my grandparents attain their high social status now flung them down the social ladder. Meiguo Ah-ma was looked down upon by the Nationalist soldiers and viewed as a traitor to her own country.

At the time, my grandmother wasn't practicing medicine because she was pregnant with her fourth child, but she did other work around the clinic. Once, a soldier came running into her clinic, complaining of an upset stomach. This much she could understand because he was doubled over, clutching his stomach, and howling loudly. A nurse who could speak Mandarin helped her diagnose the soldier's problem. My grandmother prescribed a mild pain killer for his upset stomach. The next day, the same soldier came charging into the clinic, yelling and screaming at my grandmother, accusing her of poisoning him and wanting to murder him; he claimed that the medicine she had prescribed had given him a fever. He did not stop yelling at her and would not leave the clinic until my grandmother gave him a different kind of medicine for his fever, free of charge.

All over the island, wherever the Chinese Nationalists had arrived, tension between them and the native Taiwanese began to build. The Taiwanese felt that the Nationalists didn't keep the island's immediate interests in mind and that, instead of looking to Taiwan's modernization as an example for the rest of the Republic of China, they stole from the island's resources for the temporary relief of poverty on the mainland and to help strengthen the Nationalist army, now being pushed farther and farther south by Mao's Communist Party. On the other hand, the Nationalists felt that it was time the Taiwanese were reunited with their ancestral homeland;

they had been under the influence of foreign colonizers for too long. The differences—however superficial or profound—between Taiwanese and Chinese Nationalist intentions for Taiwan's future became more and more pronounced.

On the night of February 27, 1947, a Taiwanese woman was selling contraband cigarettes on a street corner in Taipei. Nationalist investigators had heard a rumor about a large shipment of illegal matches and cigarettes earlier that day, assumed the woman's cigarettes were from that shipment, and confiscated her cigarettes and the small amount of money she had made that night. She reacted by screaming for her money back and reaching out to grab an arm of one of the investigators. A crowd had closed in on the scene. An investigator smashed the butt of his rifle into the woman's head. The crowd began to yell at the investigators, calling them pigs and a-shan, "people from the mountains," and demanded that they return the woman's cigarettes. In the confusion, gunshots were fired from an investigator's pistol. One bullet hit a bystander, who later died. The angry crowd ran to the closest police station and ordered the murderous investigator to be executed. The next morning, on February 28th, the characters—zhong guo, "China"—were stripped from signs for the China Hotel and the Bank of China and replaced by a banner in Japanese that read, "Down with Military Tyranny." In the month that followed, all the tension that had been building since Taiwan was restored to the mainland exploded into a bloodbath between the Taiwanese and the wai sheng ren, literally, "people from outside the province"—mainlanders who had emigrated to the island after Restoration. It has come to be known as the February 28th Incident, or simply, "two-two-eight."

At the time, my grandfather had a position at the Red Cross Hospital and was so busy there that Meiguo Ah-ma rarely saw him. When she did want to visit her husband, she had to walk quickly and stealthily through back alleys to get to the hospital in order to avoid the KMT soldiers, her skinny legs moving nervously down narrow alleys, one hand clutching her protruding stomach as she looked behind her to check if anyone had seen her. Meiguo Ah-ma heard about what had happened with the cigarette vendor. She knew that it would be dangerous for her to get in trouble with the soldiers now and was especially nervous about meeting any mainlanders because her elementary Mandarin would give her away as a "stupid Japanese ghost." What language you spoke on the streets revealed to which side you belonged.

On March 7, 1947, Meiguo Ah-ma gave birth to a baby boy in the basement of the Red Cross Hospital. Outside, riots had been breaking out all over the city. She remembered hearing gunshots fired throughout the night and feeling terribly fortunate to have friends in the Red Cross Hospital, some of whom were Japanese doctors who had not yet returned to Japan after the war. Was that the same night the KMT began arresting islanders at random? She couldn't remember. She couldn't keep things straight. Ever since the incident with the cigarette vendor, the whole city had seemed a volcanic eruption of violence and hatred. One terrible day blurred into the next. Had she really just given birth to a baby boy in the midst of all this?

The day after her baby was born, Meiguo Ah-ma heard that the arrests were not random. She learned that Governor Chen Yi blamed four groups for the uprising: the Communists, the Japanese who had not left Taiwan after Restoration, the new Taiwanese elite, and ordinary native Taiwanese citizens. My grandmother found out that many of her friends had been arrested. One of them was a family friend who held a high position at a prominent news agency. She learned that he had been taken away in the night and never found.

Ah-ma and my grandfather could not sleep. Every night, they wondered whether my grandfather would be the next to go. He had been a well-known doctor under the Japanese occupation, and it was no secret that he had many Japanese friends. They were afraid, too, for my grandfather's brother, who was a professed Communist reporter for a Japanese newspaper. Every day they heard about people who had been taken away, tied up with wires that cut deep into their skin, beaten to death, and then thrown into the river. A little girl who was the daughter of one of their friends came to stay with my grandparents after her father had been arrested. Hour after hour, the little girl sat with my grandparents, at once wanting to have news of her father and horrified by how awful the truth may be. My grandparents sat with her, deathly afraid that at any minute the soldiers would barge through their front door with the butts of their rifles, charge into the house, and take my grandfather away.

"Later," Meiguo Ah-ma said, closing her eyes, "there were bodies everywhere." She opened her eyes, and I saw that she was looking at me. "Some would float up to the surface of the water, and we would see that the eyes were gouged out." I had stopped taking notes and suddenly became conscious of the whirring of the tape going round and round. My grandmother looked away.

A *New York Times* article headline from March 29, 1947, reads, "Formosa killings are put at 10,000. Foreigners say the Chinese slaughtered demonstrators without provocation." The report continues:

"An American who had just arrived . . . said that troops from the mainland arrived there March 7 and indulged in three days of indiscriminate killing and looting. For a time everyone seen on the streets was shot at, homes were broken into and occupants killed. In the poorer sections the streets were said to have been littered with dead. There were instances of beheading and mutilation of bodies, and women were raped."

On March 17, 1947, Governor Chen-Yi submitted his letter of resignation to Chiang Kai-shek, not as an admission of his responsibility for the two-two-eight massacre—he claimed to have never ordered such brutal killings—but as an acknowledgment of, and regret for, the Nationalist army's unjustifiable violence toward the Taiwanese. Sources today still remain silent about who had, in fact, ordered the Nationalist troops to arrest, torture, and kill the Taiwanese people that they did. The total number of Taiwanese casualties and arrests continues to be vague. A Communist source reports that the number exceeded 50,000, while Taiwanese revolutionary organizations in Japan and the United States have made claims ranging from 10,000 to 100,000. Whatever the exact number, the Nationalists had succeeded in forcing the Taiwanese to surrender to their rule.

Somehow, life continued, as life eventually and miraculously does after extraordinary events. In 1949, the Communists won the civil war, and Mao proclaimed the birth of the People's Republic of China on the mainland. Defeated, Chiang led his Nationalists to Taiwan, where they declared the small island the Republic of China and hoped that one day, the Republic of China would once again be reunified with the mainland. In the meantime, in Taiwan, Chiang Kai-shek's government sought to bury the events spawned by two-two-eight by forbidding anyone to speak of them and forbidding anyone to speak anything other than Mandarin in public; this was martial law—anyone who dared discuss the event or speak Taiwanese would be punished. An event in which language played such an integral part suddenly became silent and hushed like a smoldering fire, hissing and sputtering and then finally, nothing.

My grandparents went back to their life. They tended to patients during the day and went to dinner parties with friends at night. On weekends, my grandfather would wake up early, fill a small cooler with ice and beer, and go fishing by the river. After he came home, he would pack a picnic basket and take Meiguo Ah-ma and all five of their children on field trips around the island. He always brought along his camera and took many pictures of his family.

The photographs I have seen from that time have an eerie, silent quality to them. Even if, in the pictures, the children are laughing and running around, their movements blurring them thin into the air, I cannot imagine the voices or the laughter. The sounds of everyday life seem to be muffled by the imposing silence of two-two-eight.

It wasn't until the late 1980s when Chiang's son, Chiang Ching-kuo, was president that martial law was lifted. Immediately, there was an outpouring of literature written about two-two-eight by people of my father's generation—people who had been children during the massacres. I asked my grandmother whether it was difficult living in such terrible silence. She had never thought about that, she told me. Maybe, she thought, it would have been even more trying to talk about two-two-eight when the emotions had been still so raw and the losses so recent and incomprehensible. Maybe, she decided, silence was time—time for everyone to heal and make sense of their world.

3.

Meiguo Ah-ma took me to my first movie. On the corner of Ho-ping and Tun-hua roads, a few blocks from our apartment in Taipei, was the Plum Blossom Theater. The plum blossom is Taiwan's national flower.

When I was young, my mother enrolled me in a Chinese calligraphy and painting class. Like writing characters, in which there is a certain order to making each stroke so as to achieve perfect balance, Chinese painting is taught in the same spirit. To paint a plum blossom, you always start with the branch by dragging your inked brush along the thin, porous paper. At different intervals, you stop, pause, and let the ink seep, spread, and bleed into the paper. These are the knuckles in the branches. It was all right if your brush became a little dry—the white parts in the markings gave the branch a three-dimensional effect. In Chinese painting, as in writing, the negative spaces are just as, if not more, important in describing something (like silences in speech). When you finish drawing the branch, you then paint the blossoms, beginning with a few dots on the inside. This is the pollen inside the flower. We were taught to make the dots loosely in the arrangement of the Chinese character for heart—xin. For the flower petals, you use an ink that is powder pink or magenta in hue. The five petals are arranged in different ways, depending on the season or mood you are describing—sometimes the blossom will be opened and inviting; other times, the blossom is shy and closed. The contrast between the delicate pink blossom and the scraggily, thick branch is what makes the plum blossom so enchanting. Meiguo Ah-ma reminds me of the plum blossom: Her frame is small and delicate—thin arms, thin legs, straight nose, soft, grey hair—but inside, she is strong and even a little hard.

My grandmother took me to the movies at the Plum Blossom Theater in the early afternoon—the time of day reserved for grandparents and young children when parents are still at work and older siblings are still in school. We walked down the block in the humid air, holding hands. On the street, vendors were selling link sausages and hot egg cakes. Meiguo Ah-ma pointed to the egg cake vendor and said we could share a bag after the movie.

As we walked up the stairs into the theater, I asked her what movie we were going to see, and she told me the title—Liang Shan-bo and Ju Ying-tai. "What does that mean?" I asked her. Those are the names of the lovers, she said. "The movie is a love story?" My grandmother nodded. It is an old Chinese love story, one of her favorites. "You've already seen it?" She nodded again, squeezing my hand.

We entered the already-darkened theater. I felt disoriented but let my grandmother lead the way and show me what to do. We walked slowly down the theater, groping our way in the darkness, Meiguo Ah-ma holding onto seat arms. The theater was near empty; there were a few black silhouettes in the dark, slumped low in their seats, thick blue smoke swirling into the air above them from the orange-lit end of their cigarettes. We sat on the left side of the theater, three rows from the big screen. I had to crane my neck to take in the whole screen. Ah-ma can't see, she explained in a whisper.

All was quiet and still except for the sound of the springs in the chairs as people shifted. Suddenly, the room became even darker, though I couldn't understand how that was possible. The darkness enveloped all of us, making it difficult even to see my grandmother sitting right next to me. Then the movie screen lit up, and I looked excitedly at Meiguo Ah-ma. She stood up from her chair. I looked around the theater, and the anonymous, genderless figures stood up in their seats, too. Meiguo Ah-ma reached down and gave my shoulder a gentle shake; I stood up. A woman's voice boomed from the loudspeaker and said in Mandarin, "The national anthem!"

I watched as the characters to Taiwan's national anthem popped up on the screen and a recording of a choir singing the anthem filled the theater and filled my ears. Behind the lyrics on the screen, there were images of different parts of the island and different people doing different things: farmers knee-deep in rice paddies; factory workers sitting at big machines; and President Chiang Ching-kuo making a speech, wearing his usual khaki windbreaker. I looked around the theater and saw people's profiles and watched as lips moved to the music. Meiguo Ah-ma's head was tilted back, and her mouth moved, too, although she sang at her own pace, in her own time. When the song was finished, the same female voice that had announced the anthem said, "Please sit down!" We sat, and the movie began.

Liang Shan-bo and Ju Ying-tai was a musical. It was a Chinese opera. The actors spoke in melodies and poetry, in an archaic Chinese that I could not understand. Thinking about it now, I know that my grandmother had not understood the language that was spoken in the movie, either. But the story unfolded before us on the actors' faces, in their expressions, their gestures, and in the music—our emotions rose on the crescendos and descended with the decrescendos. Ju Ying-tai loved Liang Shan-bo, and when he went away to university (no women were allowed to be educated in school), Ju Ying-tai disguised herself as a man so that she could be close to him. They became very close; Liang Shan-bo entrusted Ju Ying-tai with all his most private thoughts. But soon, Ju Ying-tai's real identity and sex were revealed, to Liang Shan-bo's great horror. They could not be together any longer—society wouldn't allow it. In the end, after they had both died, Liang Shan-bo and Ju Ying-tai became butterflies and fluttered away together, up into the sky.

Meiguo Ah-ma and I sat side by side in the velveteen darkness. Together, we were fluent in a wordless tongue. Even as the credits rolled up the movie screen and we heard the people behind us get up, one by one, we remained in our seats. I reached over and found my grandmother's hand.

The year I lived in San Francisco after college, I often visited Meiguo Ah-ma at her condo in San Mateo. Usually, we went to a Japanese restaurant called Sushi Sam's for lunch. She had been going to Sam's for the past fifteen years and knew Sam and his wife and all the other sushi chefs behind the counter. Whenever she walked in, setting off the little bell hanging on the door, everyone would look up and greet her in animated Japanese. Without fail, she always introduced me, patting me gently on the shoulder. "My granddaughter," she would say in English, because Sam didn't speak Chinese and I didn't speak Japanese. And then she would continue, with unrestrained pride, her head trembling slightly from side to side, "I have fifteen grandchildren!"

On one of these afternoons, after Meiguo Ah-ma and I had had lunch at Sam's and were back at her condo, she told me she had something to give to me. She disappeared into her closet for a long while. I could hear the sound of rustling plastic from the dry cleaner's swish-swishing from within the darkness. I waited on her bed and watched the hanging dresses and coats swing in and out of her closet as she maneuvered her way inside. Finally, she reemerged, carefully shuffling out backwards. She was holding a long black dress.

"See?"

I saw. It was that qi pao I had always admired in her photographs. The one she had designed, using black lace and layering it on top of a silk chemise.

I brushed my hand across the dress shyly as my grandmother pushed it into my hands.

"I think you are the size I used to be. It should fit," she said hopefully. She was now only four foot eleven and weighed just over eighty-five pounds. "Your hips are just as round as mine were." She laughed, then sighed, "but now look at me, all skin and bones." Meiguo Ah-ma helped zip me into her dress, smoothing out the lace around my shoulders. I buttoned up the long, diagonal row of buttons that ran from my left armpit across my chest to the top of the stand collar. She turned me around and looked up at me. She took a few steps back. Then she came back and lifted the hem of the dress from mid-calf to right above my knees.

"Shorter, I think, is better," she decided. She reached over to close her closet door, and we looked at my reflection in the mirror. This was the first qi pao I had tried on. I looked like someone from an old photograph. My grandmother, the top of her head barely at the top of my shoulder, stood beside me and wrapped her arm around my arm and slipped her hand into mine. I looked at her in the mirror and noticed that she was looking at me with an expression of both amusement and wistfulness—it was as though she were looking at me and saw something of her youth.

PLACE

When thinking about a place, we often have a collection of images, smells, and sounds that together form a description of that place. For example, when I think of New York City, I smell the warm, stale air around the subway platform; I see shiny, chrome bagel and coffee carts on street corners; and I hear the shrill calls of passing fire trucks. When I think of San Francisco, I see the view of Golden Gate Bridge from the skinny, silky stretch of Baker Beach and smell the cool crispness of the foggy morning air. But when I think of Taiwan, I often see just an image of my father, who for me, has always represented the epitome of pure "Taiwaneseness." The spirit of Taiwan is in his determined eyes, his loud voice that often embarrasses my mother, his emphatic gestures, and his unapologetic—sometimes brutal, often refreshing—honesty. He was born on the island, and, he tells me, he will die on the island. But had he not spent time away from Taiwan when he was in his twenties—had emigration to the United States not been a real and viable option for him and my mother—I do not think he would feel the same passion he does for Taiwan that he does now. Albert Camus once wrote, "to be pure means to rediscover that country of the soul where one's kinship with the world can be felt, where the throbbing of one's blood mingles with the violent pulsations of the afternoon sun. It is a well-known fact that we always recognize our homeland at the moment we are about to lose it." The key is in one's rediscovery of what has always been true. The act of coming back, of reacquaintance, of seeing through fresh eyes and making new something that was old and taken for granted, is the act of reclaiming and recognizing one's homeland and one's relationship to it.

This is the story and the journey of my father's coming home. It is also the beginning of the story of my own rediscovery.

1.

My father was born in Taipei in 1945, at the end of the war. His parents named him Tai-sheng, "the birth of peace." But I have always thought it more appropriate to align my father's birth with the birth of Taiwanese identity. In 1945, fifty years of Japanese occupation in Taiwan ended. And just two years after that, the February 28th Incident—the violent outbreak between native Taiwanese and the recently immigrated Chinese Nationalists—inspired Taiwanese people to begin thinking about their identity as distinct from that of people on the mainland. My father grew up in a Taipei that consisted of wet, green rice paddies and tall betelnut palms shooting into the sky. He grew up in a Taipei where three-wheeled rickshaws and the occasional big black car rolled up and down the broad, open roads. He grew up in a house on a street named after Dr. Sun Yat-sen. Almost forty years later, on top of the foundation for that family house, my father would open the largest branch of his children's clothing store.

The Taipei of my father's youth is a place I can easily picture—and smell—because he is able to describe it in great detail, with the kind of adoration and nostalgia that I have never been able to feel about the places of my own childhood. When my father talks about his childhood, he talks with bright eyes and a tone that belies both the immediacy and nostalgic distance of the past in his memory; he is self-conscious of its preciousness. I envy the wholeness of my father's childhood. If it is at all possible to be nostalgic for a past that is not one's own, I am nostalgic for the Taipei of my father's youth. I have pulled together all the fragments of stories that my father has told me and threaded them, like individual pearls on a string.

The street in front of my father's house was wide and relatively busy, where many vendors regularly hawked their snacks. After school, my father would rush home and walk back and forth in front of these vendors, trying hard to decide whether he should spend his allowance on a sweet or a salty snack. His favorite was a block of pig's blood and glutinous rice on a wooden stick, rolled around in sweet peanut powder and finely chopped cilantro. The treat was kept hot in a bamboo steamer. On days when my father wanted something sweet, he usually got a bowl of shaved ice with sweetened condensed milk drizzled over it. Sometimes he and his two brothers and sisters could add a sweet azuki bean paste to their shaved ice—an expensive Japanese touch that was difficult to come by after the war. My two uncles have told me that the reason they were always skinny—unlike my father, who was always a little pudgy—was that my father would wolf down his snacks and help himself to their unfinished treats by reaching over with his hungry hands.

At dusk, the snack vendors went home to have dinner with their families and were replaced by a man who wore thick, black-framed glasses. He spread a sheet on the ground and carefully laid out used paperback books on the sheet. He lit the two lanterns that he carried with him and placed them on either side of his book display. After dinner, my father and his brothers and sisters came outside to browse. When one of them discovered a comic book, the five children would all huddle close by one of the lanterns and laugh and point excitedly at the pictures. Bugs flew close to the light, but no one seemed to notice—certainly, no one cared. Cicadas whistled in the darkening trees by the road.

The comic books of the late 1940s and early 1950s, inspired by political cartoons, were filled with anti-Japanese sentiments. The newly established KMT government was aware that, under the Japanese, the Taiwanese had enjoyed many benefits and luxuries that Chiang Kai-shek could not provide. Chiang's biggest concern was reunification with China under the KMT. Taiwan was merely his temporary base, and his government needed Taiwanese support, which his government tried to secure through two means: spreading anti-Japanese and anti-Communist sentiment and imposing martial law. Though my father and his brothers and sisters laughed at the funny pictures in the comic books, they were too innocent to understand the deeper implications these comics contained.

The other books that the vendor sold were mostly history books. My father later found out from his parents that the book vendor was a history scholar who liked to spend his nights talking to people about his books, history, and current events—he didn't much care whether he sold his books. One day, when my father was nine, he came home from school with a difficult assignment. He had to write a speech for a school contest. He remembered the book vendor and waited eagerly all night for the vendor to lay out his books in front of the house. When my father was excused from the dinner table, he ran outside and found the vendor in his usual spot, wiping his thick glasses with the untucked part of his shirt. My father told the book vendor about his assignment and asked if he could help him with the speech. The book vendor's eyes lit up, and he nodded his head confidently and patted the top of my father's closely shaved head. The next day, the vendor showed up and handed my father a completed speech. He had gone home and written the whole thing! My father memorized the speech and won the school contest. The speech that the book vendor had written and my father delivered was about the importance of being anti-Japanese.

At the time, my father was not conscious of what that speech implied about his own family background. His parents had grown up under the Japanese occupation and had both been educated in Japan. They spoke perfect Japanese, and it wasn't until after 1945, when the Japanese withdrew from Taiwan, that they began to learn Mandarin. Even though my father learned Mandarin at school, he spoke Taiwanese with his parents at home, and his parents often spoke Japanese with each other. In many ways, his parents were more Japanese than Chinese. But the new education under the KMT, which was modeled after traditional Chinese education, tried to instill in its students an unquestioning obedience. Chinese learning was largely based on rote memorization so that a student was praised for accurate, word-for-word recitation of a text rather than for understanding the material. My father memorized the book vendor's speech with only one thought in mind: to win the contest. The content of the speech was secondary, as was its originality. It wasn't until years later, when he discovered the memorized speech could still roll off his tongue as if he had to recite it the next day, that my father realized what he had been professing to the whole school. He was amazed at his own naiveté.

The truth was, there were many contradictions between what my father was taught at school and what he knew to be true at home. He was taught to hate the Japanese, but his parents seemed part Japanese and had many Japanese friends who were all nice people. He fondly remembered the time a Japanese couple had brought a tin of butter cookies from Japan. The cookies were so good that my father hugged the empty tin when he finished the last cookie and ran around the house, announcing that he was going to marry this cookie tin when he grew up. At school, the teachers required everyone to speak Mandarin all the time, and if anyone was caught speaking Taiwanese, he had to pay a fine. But at home, my father spoke Taiwanese with his parents and his brothers and sisters.

My father's parents made sure he and his brothers and sisters grew up in a setting that did not force them to acknowledge the contradictions in their day-to-day lives under the new government. Why should the family deny that their Taiwanese identity was both Japanese- and Chinese-influenced? My father's parents wanted their children to know that they could, and should, accept their identity as inclusive of more than one culture. They were never explicit about wanting their children to dismiss some of what they learned at school, but they stressed the importance of learning from real-life experience. Above all, I think they taught my father the value of trusting and honoring his family because it would be the one constant in his life.

In 1955, my father's father died of a heart attack. My father was only ten, still too young, he told me, to comprehend sorrow. It wasn't until he was in junior high that he began to feel the pain of having lost his father and understand the magnitude of this pain. I imagine him being fatherless at so young an age and realized that this loss was what characterized my father's youth with such a mixture of mischief and an intense sense of responsibility. He was the one who stole snacks from his brothers, but also the one who stood up for his younger brother when their mother found the little one smoking a cigarette; my father claimed responsibility, saying he should have taken better care of his brother. But even though the absence of a father figure eventually became very present, that pain was never as great as the appreciation and love my father developed for his mother, who did everything on her own. She kept a portrait of her husband in the living room and taught her children that they could still communicate with their father if they looked at his portrait and talked with him quietly in their hearts. That portrait of my grandfather has been hanging in my father's study in our apartment for as long as I can remember. My father still talks with his father the way his mother taught him. Every night while I was growing up—and even now when I visit my parents in Taiwan—my father lights a stick of incense, holds it in both hands, and says a prayer to his father. I have watched him perform this ritual many times—his eyes are always closed and his thin lips move quickly, mouthing silent words; he then sticks the burning incense in a small, jade-green ceramic bowl of ashes accumulated from burnt incense of previous nights and retires to bed.

I remember when I was about ten I asked my father, after he had said his "prayers" one night, "Daddy, what religion are we?" I knew that Meiguo Ah-ma was Christian because after my grandfather died, a couple who were friends of hers had tried to console her with religion. They approached her—the wife with a Chinese book on Buddhism, the husband with a Japanese book on Christianity—and because my grandmother's Japanese was far superior to her Chinese, she chose Christianity. My mother's mother, Taichung Ah-ma, had been a devout Buddhist. Neither grandmother had ever imposed her religion on her children, and so my parents followed their example of granting us religious freedom. But I was completely ready to embrace my family's religion. I did not question; I just needed my father to tell me what to believe in. My father looked at the picture of his father and answered, "I believe in our family." He put his thick, calloused hand on my shoulder and pushed it down firmly. The gesture told me that my father was teaching me something of great significance. That I had asked the question made me worthy of knowing the answer—the source of our family's faith.

Family members, my father taught me, have to learn to trust one another. This is an ongoing process, one that is not always easy, but when you believe in your family and your family believes in you, you will feel the freedom and the strength to do anything you aspire to. My father told me that I could go wherever I wanted to go as long as I was rooted in the place where I was from. And this place was not a geographical place. It was family—that unwavering little nugget of faith in my heart that told me that stability would grant me mobility.

2.

For eight years—from high school through college and one year of compulsory military service—my father played competitive rugby (so different from the usual sports we associate with the Taiwanese—badminton, table tennis, and baseball). Playing so often in the sun gave his complexion a dark, reddish tone. He developed bulging, angular muscles in his arms and legs. Over the eight-year period, he broke three bones—his collarbone, one of his ribs, and a bone in his leg. I remember seeing a photograph of him when his leg was broken. He was leaning easily on crutches—as if he didn't need them—and laughing at the camera with his mouth wide open. In the picture, my father was wearing a sweater that my mother had knitted for him. When I squinted closely at the photograph, I saw that there was a short moustache above my father's lip. His eyebrows then were thick and black. Now they are long and white and hang over his eyes. Chinese tradition tells us that long eyebrows are a sign of wisdom, and superstition warns that it would be bad luck to trim them. My mother once bought my father a little tube of clear mascara so that he could brush his eyebrows out of his eyes, but he never uses it.

My father used to laugh and ask whether my brother and I were surprised that someone as elegant and refined as our mother could fall for someone like him. "Daddy is such a simple and rough man," he would say. But when we were young, my brother and I wondered the opposite—we asked why someone as tough and exciting as our father would fall for our mother, who was studious and quiet and liked to spend her time in art museums. We were mesmerized by our father's commanding presence when he walked into a room. He was often the center of attention, telling jokes with his loud, bellowing voice, and was always the first to laugh after he'd delivered the punch line. His audience usually responded to the excitement with which he told a story rather than to the story itself. I could tell that even my father's friends were captivated by him, which delighted me a great deal because it was a confirmation from the outside (and adult) world that the person I considered unique was actually unique.

Sometime when he was in college, in the late '60s, my father began to grow a full beard. Most Taiwanese men don't have enough facial hair to do that, but my father grew a beard he had to trim often. His friends gave him the nickname Hu Zi, "Beard." Later, one of my mother's American friends gave her a plaque that read, "Kissing a man without a beard is like eating an egg without salt." Even after the brass plate mounted on the wooden plaque had tarnished, my father kept it displayed proudly on the shelf in his study.

People on the streets often stared at him with a bewildered look on their faces, wondering if he was a foreigner. One night my father went bowling with some friends. The people in the bowling alley gave him inquisitive looks, but he ignored them. He had just hit a strike and yelled, "Zan!"—"Super!"—in Taiwanese. His voice boomed and echoed all across the lanes. Suddenly, two police officers showed up by his side. They grabbed his arms.

"What are you doing?" my father shouted, looking at the officers on either side of him.

"We thought you were a foreigner," one of the officers said in Mandarin, looking at my father suspiciously, "until we heard you speak Taiwanese!"

"I am Taiwanese!" My father successfully twisted one arm out of one officer's grip. The officer quickly grabbed hold of his arm again, this time with both hands. "What are you doing?" My father demanded again.

"If you are Chinese," the officer corrected, "then you should know that you are not allowed to have a beard on your face!"

"Are you kidding?" My father looked around at his friends, who surrounded him and the officers in a timid semicircle. "Are they kidding?"

"It's martial law," said one of the officers sternly.

"What?! I didn't know there were laws against having a beard! This is ridiculous! You don't have the right to dictate how I should or shouldn't look!"

"Oh, yes we do," said the officer. "It's the law."

"Yeah? Show me where this law is written."

The police officers gave each other confused looks. One of them narrowed his eyes and tilted his head toward the front door of the bowling alley. "All right. Then you're coming with us to the police station."

"Fine," my father said through his teeth.

When they got to the station, the officers threw my father into a cell and locked him up. They made no move to show my father where it was written that a person was not allowed to wear a beard. One policeman pushed his face between two iron bars and told my father that he'd better shave off his beard. My father refused. He waited for a few hours. Finally, he asked, "Eh! How long are you going to keep me here? I can't stay here all night, you know."

"You will stay as long as you have your beard!"

Every time my father retells the end of this story, I am disappointed because the truth is anticlimactic. I can tell that my father wishes he could end it with the scene of him behind bars, with a full beard and his arms folded angrily, heroically across his chest. But eventually, the officers gave my father two choices: He could pay ten yuan for a barber to come shave his beard, or he could shave it off himself and be released. He chose the latter and went home, though he was determined to grow his beard again.

I think my father had been arrested that night for speaking Taiwanese in public. But my father told me he was sure he was arrested for simply having a beard on his face because martial law under the KMT had become more and more absurd. The KMT repressed Taiwanese culture and identity in any way they saw fit in order to force the native Taiwanese to accept its new Chinese government. For nearly four decades, the people on Taiwan were subjected to this awkward and unreasonable political arrangement, and it became the longest period of uninterrupted martial law in modern history. The prospect of Chiang Kai-shek not being able to reunite Taiwan with China under KMT rule was every day becoming more apparent, and the Taiwanese were not oblivious to the fact that Chiang still did not care about developing the island and that he used Taiwan's resources and manpower to fuel his ultimate goal of returning to the mainland.

In 1968, at the age of twenty-four, my father left Taiwan for Fresno, California. He had studied psychology at the National Taiwan University and wanted to get his master's in the United States. My mother, who was a year older than my father, had already taken a month-long boat ride the preceding year to San Francisco. In the year my parents left for America, which is now known as Taiwan's "brain drain," almost twenty percent of college graduates from the top schools in Taiwan left home to study abroad, and only five percent of them returned to Taiwan. There was an intense feeling of uncertainty about Taiwan's future. People feared that Mao would "wash Taiwan with blood" to make the island a part of Communist China. And they also feared that Chiang would continue to rule Taiwan without regard to the island's immediate interests and insist upon laws that tried to control Taiwanese people's thoughts, actions, and appearances. In the late '60s, everyone encouraged everyone else to leave if their families could afford to. Because both my grandmothers were doctors, they had enough money saved so that members of their families could begin packing their bags to move to the United States.

The KMT government encouraged students to emigrate and study abroad. The regular outflow of some of Taiwan's best college students provided them with a safety valve—these students were the very people the KMT expected to be at the core of any activist movement. Without them, there was a smaller chance that Chiang Kai-shek's regime would be challenged.

In Fresno, my father concentrated on his schoolwork during the week, and on the weekends he drove a secondhand, white Volkswagen Beetle to San Francisco to see my mother. (They had started dating when they were in college.) In San Francisco, my parents took long walks together, went to the beach, and ate at Taco Bells. To this day, when my parents come to the States for a visit, they insist on stopping by at Taco Bell for a plate of nachos and some tacos and always say that they used to make them much better. Photographs of my parents during this time always surprise me. In particular, there's one of my parents leaning against the Bug—my father's arm is thrown casually around my mother's shoulders, and my mother's arm is raised to push the hair out of her eyes. They look so young and yet already so much like my parents. On the back of the photograph, both my parents have written their own captions for the picture, referring to each other by their pet names.

I like seeing my parents in their twenties, in the context of 1960s America—they look independent and free, and I can see myself in their faces, as I am now in my mid-twenties and am every day surprised by this consciousness of being on the brink of something, of being in the midst of growing up. I can read from my parents' body language and from their smiles in the pictures that they were already in love. They were already in love in the certain, assured way they are today. I suppose that is why—even with my mother's long hair, miniskirts, and big sunglasses and my father's clean-shaven face (by the time I was born, he had grown his beard again and has not shaved it since)—they already look like my parents in those photographs.

Two years in graduate school went by quickly. My father couldn't finish his master's thesis because it was too difficult for him to write the entire paper in English. This was something I did not find out until I was filling out information about my parents' educational background for my own college applications. I had gone to my mother for the information, and she instructed me to write "BA and graduate studies" on the blank line after "Father's education."

"Isn't that just an MA?" I asked.

"No," she said, "because he didn't finish his thesis." As I penciled in "graduate studies" so I could type it in later, my mother added quickly while grabbing my arm, "But don't tell him I told you. It upsets him when he's reminded of it." My mother is always protecting my father like that. There is an image of him that she likes to keep—one that is the product of all the lessons he has learned and not of the mistakes he's made.

So in the spring of 1970, instead of getting his master's diploma, my father married my mother in a modest reception hall in Fresno. My mother's roommate, Brenda Hunt (after whom I was named), played the organ, and Brenda's sister baked their cake. Only family and a few close friends attended the ceremony; this helps me imagine my parents' small and intimate world at the time—their life together was unfettered by complication. That summer, my parents went on their three-month honeymoon, backpacking across Europe. They felt exhilarated to know they had their whole lives ahead of them but could bask in the suspense of these three months before they had to decide where they would settle down and what they each would do about a career.

My parents' honeymoon took them through Spain, Portugal, and finally, England. After they flew back to California, already wistful for their time in Europe and still high from the freedom of traveling, the two decided on an impulse to move to Hawaii.

When my father had still been in college in Taiwan, his mother had often invited foreign exchange students to stay at their house. She liked to expose her children to all different kinds of people and cultures. One of the exchange students, Philip Deters from Hawaii, kept in touch with my father's family. Phil wrote my grandmother often and repeatedly invited her children to stay with him in Hawaii. In the fall of 1971, my parents accepted Phil's invitation.

For six months, my parents like to say now, they "bummed around" in Hawaii. My mother, who had gotten her degree in biological sciences, easily found a job working in a laboratory. It was an easy environment for her to work in because she could spend most of her days quietly conducting experiments. And even in social situations, my mother was comfortable because her English was good. She had always had a knack for languages and was never shy about using phrases she'd picked up in conversation, even if the syntax might be a bit off (my favorite: "Well, let us play it by the ear!").

My father, on the other hand, experienced difficulties. It was almost impossible for him to find a job, even with a degree in psychology, especially because any job in the field required him to converse a lot in English. He ended up working as part of a maintenance crew in a hotel, shampooing carpets and waxing floors. His shift started at six in the morning and ended at two in the afternoon. After work, he put on a colorful Hawaiian shirt or a Mexican guayabera, khaki shorts, and slippers and strolled onto the beach to wait for my mother to get off work at four.

My parents' time in Hawaii was different from their time in Europe. In Hawaii, my father was close enough to the mainland United States to feel, with increasing certainty, that he could not stay in America. There were too many barriers he felt he could not break through to feel at home there. He could not speak the language without feeling embarrassed and restrained. How was he to tell jokes when he couldn't—with his usual confidence, style, and good timing—deliver the punch line in English as well as he could in Taiwanese and Mandarin?

Once, one of my cousins told my father a joke about a group of friends who wanted to go camping. Each person was assigned to bring a specific item for the trip; the Chinese man in the group was supposed to bring the supplies. On the day when the group planned to meet with all their gear for the camping trip, everyone was there except the Chinese man. Just as everyone looked around, wondering where he was, the Chinese man jumped out from behind some bushes—where he had been hiding—with his arms stretched up excitedly and yelled, "SUPPLIES!!"

My cousin laughed after she finished telling the joke, and my father looked at her blankly. "Right," he said in Chinese. "Supplies. . . ." he muttered in English, unimpressed with the joke because he did not get it. And that set my cousin off laughing even harder. Then I saw the expression on my father's face—his thick eyebrows were knotted in confusion, and his eyes betrayed some acknowledgment that he had unwittingly become the butt of the joke. I was angry with my cousin for making my father play the part of the Chinese man in that joke.

In Hawaii, my father was also far away enough from Taiwan to know that he was nostalgic for home. After traveling to so many places in the world, he knew that there was a real passion for home, which he would never feel for another place. I don't think my parents were delaying their plans for the future by spending those six months in Hawaii. They weren't just "bumming around." My father needed the time and that unique place that had a comfortable distance from both mainland United States and Taiwan for him to know what he wanted: To come home.

At the end of their six months in Hawaii, my parents decided to move back to Taiwan. Phil gave them a book of photographs of the Hawaiian islands as a good-bye present. It was a book I loved looking through when I was young. I loved smelling the mustiness of its stiff, hard pages and brushing my hand across the ochres and oranges of these 1970s pictures, imagining what those six months in Hawaii were like, and inserting little black silhouettes of my parents into the photographs of sunsets and sunrises. I like knowing that there was a time when my parents were confused and searching for answers and entirely uncertain about their future. I like knowing that this time was spent in Hawaii, where my father shampooed carpets and my mother worked in some nameless, descriptionless lab, and that they spent their afternoons by the water, hand in hand, unafraid by this uncertainty because they had each other.

By the end of those six months, both of my parents' families had emigrated to San Francisco and New York. Everyone in their families had decided to leave Taiwan just as my parents boarded the plane to settle down in the home that my father would never want to leave again.

3.

My parents returned to Taiwan in 1971. It was the same year President Nixon accepted an invitation to visit the People's Republic of China—a trip that changed the United States' policy toward China and Taiwan. Before Nixon went to China, Taiwan had a seat in the United Nations and official diplomatic ties with most countries in the world; Taiwan enjoyed open trade relations with the United States. Soon after Nixon announced that the United States had decided to establish diplomatic relations with China, adopting the "one China policy," Taiwan was forced to withdraw from the United Nations. By 1972, most countries cut off diplomatic relations with Taiwan in favor of China. Today, only twenty-five mostly small (and well compensated) countries recognize Taiwan.

Chiang Ching-kuo took over his father's rule in 1972. He was different from his father in that he inspired efforts in the KMT government to develop Taiwan for Taiwan's sake, not just in the hope of reunification with China. He appointed Lee Teng-hui, a native-born Taiwanese, as his vice president. The political situation on the island was beginning to improve, but when my mother was pregnant later that year with my brother, she and my father both agreed that Taiwan's future was still not secure enough to make their children Taiwanese citizens. They would wait until their children were older and let them decide on their own if they wanted to become Taiwanese citizens. So in the beginning of the following year, my mother flew to New York and stayed with my father's sister in Forest Hills. My brother, Alex, was born in May 1973, and as soon as my mother and the baby were strong enough to travel, she took Alex right back to Taiwan with his American passport and birth certificate tucked safely into her luggage.

Before my mother got back, my father had started looking for jobs in the human resources departments of large companies, certain that his psychology background would help in this field. One of the first interviews he went to was at Texas Instruments, an American company that had opened a branch office in Taipei as part of Chiang Ching-kuo's new government's campaign to encourage foreign investment. My father sauntered casually into his interview with Mr. Eddie Mou, a tall, thin man who had a long face and sad, drooping eyes. Mr. Mou was about fifteen years older than my father. My father was wearing a Hawaiian shirt with a loud, colorful floral print, khaki pants, and loafers with no socks. His beard was thick, and he needed a haircut. He had been trying to grow out his hair so that he could get a perm. He wanted an Afro. Had my mother been around, she would have made sure he looked more presentable at a job interview. Several years later, when he wasn't home one afternoon, she took the liberty of throwing away all of my father's Hawaiian shirts and guayaberas.

Anyone else would probably not have given my father a chance that day. But something in my father's confidence and spirited energy told Mr. Mou not to dismiss him. The two of them ended up talking about my father's recent travels to Europe and his stay in Hawaii. Mr. Mou asked my father about his studies at school. He did not press and ask why my father had not finished his master's degree. They talked for almost two hours, and my father had not even noticed. At the end of the interview, the two men stood up, and Mr. Mou extended his arm to my father across his desk. He congratulated my father, "You got the job." Mr. Mou walked my father to the door, and when they said good-bye, he told my father, "Please, call me Eddie." Uncle Eddie, as I came to call him, was my father's mentor and became his good friend.

Imagining the circumstances of that interview now—what my father wore, his youthful assuredness, and why Uncle Eddie hired him on the spot—I see the irony of my father's return to Taiwan, to an environment that was familiar and home to him, where he could speak the language and was already a part of the cultural fabric of Taiwanese life, only to be offered a job, in part, because of his Americanness. Of course, Uncle Eddie must also have appreciated my father's devotion to Taiwan and his family. He was impressed that my father could so naturally integrate his experiences from home and abroad.

By the time my mother had returned to Taiwan with their newborn baby boy, my father had already started working for Texas Instruments, and the three of them moved into an apartment on the fourteenth floor of a cream-colored building called the Champagne Building on Zhong Xiao East Road. Uncle Eddie told my father that because TI was an American company, my father could be considered an American working abroad and work toward getting his American citizenship. My father knew that he should apply to become an American—an American passport was like a magic talisman, providing the safety and security that his Taiwanese passport could not at that time. In 1976 when my mother was pregnant with me, she took Alex with her and flew to San Francisco, where her parents were living. The three of us lived in San Francisco for almost four years while waiting for my mother to get her American "talisman."

It is difficult for me to imagine how my parents spent those four years apart, and yet I find that I often gravitate toward that specific period in my parents' life and wonder about the everyday difficulties of a young couple trying to build something together when they are so far apart. How could there not have been a question in their minds whether they were doing the right thing, whether sacrificing this time together was truly going to be worth while in the future? They had both just turned thirty; had they already begun to shed the selfishness of youth in exchange for the wisdom and generosity that I'd always assumed parents just had, miraculously? Will I feel this way, have this much foresight in a few years?

During their four years apart, my father flew to San Francisco once every three months and stayed for only a couple of weeks at a time. In the fall of 1976, when my mother was in her last months of pregnancy with me, her younger sister, Nancy, lived with us, helping my mother around the house. Auntie Nancy told me that my father flew in from Taiwan the morning of September 6, just barely making it in time for my arrival.

When I imagine the long months of my father's absence, I marvel that my mother never talks about the loneliness of those four years. Was there never any resentment? After I was born, she started working in a lab again. Every morning, she took Alex to school, dropped me off at Fan Tai Tai's, and then went to work. On the weekends, we went to my mother's parents' house or went with my uncles, aunts, and cousins on my father's side to picnic on the beach in Half Moon Bay. Once, we went horseback riding; it was very windy, and I lost the red satin ribbon that my mother had so tenderly tied onto my pigtails earlier that morning.

Sometimes my mother took all the kids to the kidney-shaped

swimming pool down the street from our house. My cousins, brother, and I splashed around in the shallow end, sitting on the first step as my mother watched from one of the mint-green, plastic lawn chairs by the pool. Once, my mother took turns carrying each of us on her back as she glided out into the middle of the pool, bobbing us up and down, in and out of the water, holding on tightly to our little hands. She was still on her way back from the middle of the pool with my cousin Margie when I decided to reach out and swim to her even though I didn't know how to swim yet. I wanted to be able to feel the warmth of the sun on her shoulder again and smell the chlorine in her damp hair. But as I pushed off the step and leapt toward my mother, I discovered that I had miscalculated the distance between us. Opening my mouth to shout out her name, I swallowed a big gulp of water instead, reached my arms up for her, and sank, slowly. Underwater, I could see the bottom half of my mother's black one-piece swimsuit and her pale, thin legs moving toward me. But she was moving as if in slow motion, creating millions of tiny bubbles every time she picked up her legs. I squeezed my eyes shut and thought maybe no one had seen me fall to the bottom of the pool. But before I reached the tiled floor, I felt my mother's arms circle me and lift me up, and we broke through the surface of the pool together. I began to cry, simultaneously trying to hold my mother as tightly as I could and hitting her with my balled up fists. She patted my back gently and started humming a familiar Japanese song close by my ear, its flats and sharps haunting, yet surprisingly soothing, too. Together, we waded out of the pool.

In my mind, I see my mother at that time—she is the only clear figure, surrounded by a blur of movement and frenzy, going through each day with a quiet determination. In the midst of rescuing me from the bottom of the pool and dropping me off at Fan Tai Tai's and taking my brother to school, she was all the time working and cooking and straightening up the house and waiting for that precious American citizenship. It is the only time that I can picture my mother without my father. Probably because we are both women, it is my mother's possible loneliness that I fixate on—more so than I do my father's. When I press my mother now and ask her to tell me how she survived being alone for those four years, she only tells me, "I can't tell you how I lived through those days because all I know is that we did what we had to do then, and now, here we all are." No regrets, and don't look back. In our family, we don't dwell on hardships, only triumphs and the right decisions.

Meanwhile, my father lived in Taipei by himself. Uncle Eddie had encouraged him to quit his job at Texas Instruments to start up his own business. He told my father that the newly opened market in Taiwan was perfect for entrepreneurs and assured my father that he had what it would take to start his own business. It was a big risk, but it was a risk my father was willing to take. When he was deciding what industry to go into, he consulted his mother. Because Meiguo Ah-ma had once been a pediatrician, her suggestion to him was, "There will always be babies." So my father borrowed money from his mother and, in partnership with another businessman, opened a shop selling baby care products. Before long, the partner decided he had better move his family to the United States, where everyone else was flocking, and where he believed there were more opportunities than Taiwan could ever offer. So he moved to New Jersey and ended up running a Hallmark card shop for the next twenty years.

Left alone with the business, my father decided to recruit friends. He made my godmother—my mother's best friend, Susan—a vice president and asked my mother if she would be the other vice president of the company as soon as she came home. The third person my father turned to was an old man, whom he called Yu Gong Gong, "Grandfather Yu," he had met through his former partner. Yu Gong Gong was my grandparents' age. He had a skinny face with sunken cheeks and large ears that looked as though they might touch his shoulders. He had puffy bags under his drooping, gray eyes, and in his shirt pocket, he always carried a bunch of stubby, yellow no. 2 pencils. I never knew what Yu Gong Gong's exact position was in the company. He became a father figure to my father, and sometimes, I think, he was like an anchor for the company and my father.

But even with all the help my father was getting from Susan and Yu Gong Gong, it could not have been easy to start this business while his family lived on another continent, thousands of miles away. Those four years my parents were separated was a time in their lives that my father never liked to discuss because he could not bear the question of whether he had made the right decision for his family. I believe that neither of my parents dwell on that past because it was so difficult and because by refusing to talk of hardships, they have finally lost the vocabulary to describe those particular emotions. Now my father claims to have forgotten how hard that time was. What does it matter, he is actually saying, when we've made it here together?

Right before Christmas in 1978, two years before my mother, brother, and I moved back to Taiwan permanently, President Jimmy Carter announced on national television his decision to establish official diplomatic ties with China and, in effect, break off ties with Taiwan. I remember very clearly that the Carter announcement was a chapter in one of the Taiwanese school primers that my Chinese tutor used for my brother and me—complete with a list of vocabulary words to learn at the end of the chapter. I cannot remember now what words were in that list, but there must have been something synonymous with "betrayal." And yet, just two years after the United States decided to favor China over Taiwan, leaving the island's future with graver uncertainties, my mother packed our bags, and the three of us flew from San Francisco to Taipei, where my father was eagerly awaiting us.

4.

When my family was reunited in Taipei in 1980, my brother, who had already completed the first grade when we were in San Francisco, was enrolled in an American school. My parents decided that we should have a bicultural education, attending the American school in the day and taking Chinese lessons at home at night. I still had two years before I could enter the first grade, so my parents put me in a Taiwanese kindergarten. Everyone there called me by my Chinese name. I don't think I even told anyone that I had been born in America or that I knew how to speak English. It wasn't so much that I was ashamed as that I wanted to be just like everyone else. But I distinctly remember the day my Americanness began to mean something to me.

My mother and I were walking home one day; the sidewalk was empty except for another mother-daughter pair walking toward us. The other girl was about the same height as I was, and we both had our arms bent in just about the same angle while holding our mothers' hands. When we came almost face to face, our eyes locked and something was understood between us—in that instant, we both knew we each had to prove that we were better than the other in some way. She immediately looked up at her mother and asked loudly in Chinese, "Mama, can we go home and play with all my new dolls?" By now, we had passed each other, and she turned around and shot a look at me: beat that.

I spun my head around and tugged my mother's hand, and though I cannot remember what I had said exactly, I know that I said it in perfect English. I smiled smugly and turned around. The little girl's head was twisted around as she continued walking with her mother, holding her hand. Her eyes were opened wide, and her jaw had dropped so low her chin was touching the top of her shoulder. Clearly, my Americanness was worth more than her new dolls. In the 1980s, anything even remotely American was deemed cool. I realized for the first time how the American part of my identity was like a trump card—something I could pull out and show off whenever I needed to.

From then on, I often pleaded with my mother to tell me stories about the time we had spent in San Francisco. I was too young to have many memories of my own, and I needed the details to round out who I was. My mother was vague, of course, because in refusing to think about those four years, both she and my father had diluted their memories of that time. All she could describe was our house and the backyard, with which I became fascinated, because in Taipei there was so little space that having your own backyard was a luxury even the rich could not easily enjoy. Soon, that backyard with its tire swing and scattered, crunchy leaves became the epitome of Americanness for me. I rummaged through old photographs and found ones of my brother and his friends playing in a red tent in the backyard. In that series, I am always on the periphery. But that did not make me feel less a part of the memories from our time in the States, which I began to reconstruct for myself using those pictures. That I was actually in the photos confirmed my American identity, and that delighted me.

That backyard was so much more appealing—and more apt to be the setting for my childhood memories—than our third-floor apartment in Taipei. There was an empty lot next to our building, but it was fenced off, and our parents told us that soon, the lot would become a large hotel with an indoor mall, which didn't impress me at all. There was a big, orange mechanical crane in the middle of that lot, and it remained there, its crooked, motionless arm in midair, for eight years. Stray dogs roamed around in the lot, and my brother and I would sometimes open the window in our kitchen and have contests to see whose fake barks could attract the dogs' attention. We lived next to the Plum Blossom movie theater, where Meiguo Ah-ma took me to see my first movie. But I didn't find that very exciting when I compared it to what I could be doing in our American backyard. My kindergarten didn't even have a playground. We ran around in the dark basement, which doubled as the music room. In short, nothing about my childhood in Taipei seemed to measure up to our backyard in San Francisco. I felt cheated, and my childhood felt fragmented.

As my time to begin first grade in the American school came closer and I showed more signs of eagerly wanting to embrace my American education, my father tried to ground me first in my Taiwaneseness. At home, he taught me how to speak Taiwanese. I already knew some phrases, because next to Japanese, my grandparents were most comfortable speaking Taiwanese. Whenever I called my father at work, he would ask me to recite the numbers in Taiwanese. I would sit on the chair next to our telephone stand, my legs dangling, kicking back and forth to the rhythm of my own counting. I would stop when I couldn't count any higher, and my father would help out. Then he told me that I had a wonderful pronunciation and it made him happy whenever I spoke our dialect. At home, my parents spoke to each other in Taiwanese, and I listened hard to know what they talked about. With time, my ear grew accustomed to Taiwanese, and I could understand almost everything.

After I started going to the American school, I noticed that my parents were very seldom involved with my schoolwork. This was partly because they were increasingly busy with the company, which now had its own clothing line and branch shops opening up in Taipei, and partly because of the language barrier. But mostly, it was because they cared more about what we learned at home. Knowing how to speak Taiwanese was one example, as was knowing how to read and write in Chinese. But even more important to my parents was that while we enjoyed the freedom and independence of an American education (we wouldn't have to endure the grueling process of entrance examinations, nor would physical punishment be customary in the classroom), we were well-versed in the traditional values of a Taiwanese household. This meant that we upheld the proper code of relationships within the family: Always treat your parents with the utmost respect and never talk back or raise your voice. That last part about not talking back was sometimes confused with not talking at all. Communication in our family was extremely nuanced, based in large part on body language, facial expressions, and inferences; rarely was communication direct discourse. This silence made growing up an often difficult and lonely process.

When I was nine years old, my mother went to Japan for a week on a business trip to collect ideas for the next season's clothing designs. It was the same week I began menstruating. I distinctly remember that after I found the rust-colored spot on my underwear, I marched mechanically into my parents' bedroom, passed my father by the door, and locked myself in their bathroom. I found my mother's box of sanitary napkins in its usual spot in the wooden cabinet. The box was pink, and the characters for "safe" and "free" floated prettily across the surface. I opened up the box and took out a napkin and pressed it into my underwear as if I had been practicing for this moment all my life. I heard my father's voice outside the door, asking timidly whether I needed help. He must have figured out what was going on, or else there would not have been any hesitancy in his tone. I told him no, and when I was finished, I marched right back out of his bathroom and my parents' bedroom, and it wasn't until I reached my room and could close and lock the door behind me that I fell onto the floor and started to cry. I cried because I was only nine, and I knew that my girlhood was already over. From that moment, I began to feel shame for the changes that were taking place in my body—a feeling that most girls at the time didn't consider until they were at least twelve or thirteen, and even then, they must have been reassured that these changes were natural and beautiful, or so I assumed from reading books like *Are You There God? It's Me, Margaret.*

At dinner that night, my father, my brother, and I sat around the table in silence. My brother, Alex, was reading a book, as he often did during dinner when he was in middle school. My father asked him to put the book away, and then the three of us continued to not talk. I know that my father had heard me crying in my room. Certainly, he could see that my eyes were swollen and the skin under my nose was red and raw from wiping. But he didn't ask me what was wrong, and in a bizarre way, I was thankful for it. When my mother returned from her Japan trip, it was assumed that I had taken care of myself and that there was nothing more we needed to discuss. And so, every month when I got my period, I endured it in private; and the secrecy and shame which surrounded this otherwise natural phenomenon made me feel that there was something terribly wrong with me but that I should accept my fate quietly.

When I reached middle school, I did try to rebel against this code of silence in our family. In the sixth grade, I started to bring home math tests with marks of seventy or below. Because my grades were so low, my teacher required that I correct my mistakes and have one of my parents sign the test, which was the part I dreaded most because my father never just signed the test. I had to sit beside him on the living room couch and wait for him to flip through the entire test. He would become increasingly impatient as he turned the pages more and more forcefully when he saw the kinds of mistakes I had made. His face would get red as he held my test in one hand and tapped it angrily with the back of his other hand and say, "But these are all careless mistakes."

"Exactly!" I would retort. "It's not like I don't know how to do these problems. I was just careless."

To which my father would say so loudly that I would jump in my seat, "Which is precisely why you should not have made any mistakes!"

These kinds of exchanges happened a few more times, each one escalating to a higher intensity, until one night, after I had talked back to my father one too many times, he looked at me furiously, raised his arm, and slapped my left cheek with an anger and force I had never seen my father display toward anyone—and especially not toward me, his xiao bao, "little treasure!" I saw the blurred images of my mother and brother somewhere behind him. Holding my burning cheek, I bore my eyes into my father's face, trying to show him how much I hated him at that moment. He did not soften. Instead, he told me to go to my room and write down what had happened in my journal so that I could learn from this experience and make sure it never happened again.

I locked myself in the bathroom with my journal, but I had no idea what lesson I was supposed to have learned. I couldn't understand why my doing well in math was so important to my father. Afterward, no one talked again about what had happened, and we each took away from it what we wanted. At the time, I was left with the notion that my father had become a rigid and unreasonable man, and as a result of that conclusion, I decided I would stop talking to him altogether. He didn't give me any reason why he had hit me that night, and I wouldn't give him any explanation of why he deserved my silent treatment. If I was in the living room and he walked in, I would stand up and leave. Sometimes I could feel my father's sad, imploring eyes on me when I made my move to leave. I knew I was hurting him, and when I was alone in my room, I considered the possibility that maybe he wanted to apologize for hitting me but that he just didn't have the words. I wanted to stop punishing myself by punishing my father, too, but I also felt as though I had never been given the faculties to utter these feelings in so many words.

Then one night after I had gotten into bed, I noticed that my father was later than usual coming home. I still had not fallen asleep an hour later when I heard the fumbling of keys. Our apartment was small enough so that I could clearly hear the clanging of metal keys against our metal apartment door. My father seemed to be having some trouble. Immediately, I saw a sliver of yellow light underneath my door as my mother turned on the living room lights and heard her quickly shuffling in her slippers to the door. When she turned the lock and opened the door, I heard her gasp, then heard her whispering. And after the door shut, I heard a deep moan from my father. He was crying.

Without thinking, I threw my blanket onto the floor and got out of bed. When I opened my door, I saw my parents sitting on the couch—my mother was holding my father in her arms, and my father's head was resting heavily on her chest and his shoulders were shaking. They looked up and saw me standing by my door, frightened and worried. My father called my name, and I immediately walked over and reached out for him. He said, "Yu Gong Gong died," and tears streamed down his face in tiny rivulets. I squeezed in between my mother and father, and at that moment of physical contact, we exchanged a flood of emotions, though not a single word.

In retrospect, I think that the math incident made apparent to my father the stark differences in our education. I realize now that math was the only way my father could be involved with my schoolwork—there was no language barrier with numbers and multiplication signs. He was perhaps overly enthusiastic in his involvement with my math assignments because he knew this was the one subject he could help me with. He was not angry that I was not proficient in math but angry that my education had taught me to be disrespectful enough to talk back to my own father. To him, that was evidence of my not honoring the family. To me, it was a natural (and American?) instinct to stand up for myself, even if it would mean questioning an older person's authority. But the reasons my father hit me that night were much more complex than my talking back to him. If talking and not talking were simplified descriptions of American and Taiwanese cultures, then my father must also have been afraid that I had made a choice about wanting to be more American than Taiwanese. And if this were true, he knew he could not fault me for this inclination because, after all, it had been his decision to make sure my brother and I were born American citizens. But the sincere hope that my brother and I would eventually declare ourselves Taiwanese citizens was one which my father never voiced. He had promised on the days we were born that this was a choice we would make for ourselves.

5.

When my father made the decision to make us American citizens, it was because no one could foresee that Taiwan would become the economically stable and affluent country that it was in the 1980s. But even though Chiang Ching-kuo was open about advancing Taiwan's economy, he was still closed to opening relations with China. Visitation between Taiwan and the mainland was prohibited until Chiang's death in 1988. I was in the sixth grade when President Chiang died. I remember seeing his face on the cover of *Time* magazine, superimposed on a map of Taiwan. I was seeing Taiwan in a context much larger than Taiwan itself. For the first time, I thought about Taiwan's role in the world at large. Before then, I had not even considered the fact that other countries did not recognize us—that, technically, the country of Taiwan did not exist. During the summers, when I went to camp with my cousins in the States and kids at camp asked, "Where?" when I told them I was from Taiwan (which was often followed by, "Oh, Thailand!"), I did not think how their ignorance might be representative of how little most people knew about Taiwan. Even people in China had very limited knowledge about Taiwan.

In 1988, my father, my mother, and a group of friends made their first trip to the mainland. At that time, the Chinese were still under the impression that Taiwanese people were backward—they had heard that when the Taiwanese ate bananas, they ate the skin, too, because they were so poor. In fact, Taiwan had been prospering under a new economy, and when the Chinese saw that the islanders traveled well and dressed well, they were surprised. On that trip, my father told me, there was very little hostility between the Chinese and the Taiwanese—mostly just genuine curiosity and warm welcome. He felt nothing more than a tourist traveling to a place he'd never been. The only difference was that he could point out some similarities between Chinese and Taiwanese culture—food, language, and a certain amount of reservation when people first met. In the end, he had no feeling of belonging when he was on the mainland. When he returned home, my father felt more Taiwanese than ever before. China was not for my father, as it was for many people living in Taiwan, his homeland.

When it came time for me to make my first trip to the mainland, my father tried to warn me that it would not be an easy trip for me. My boyfriend, Billy, and I planned to leave in mid-January of 1999. He would be finished with his last semester at Berkeley, and I would have completed my term working at an art gallery in San Francisco. During a family reunion in Monterey over New Year's, my father said to me, "People are going to look at you and know that you are not Chinese, and they will discriminate against you."

Not Chinese? I'd thought. He continued, "And what's more, you will be traveling with a foreigner. People will see a Chinese girl together with an

American man, and they won't like that." Suddenly, next to Billy's brown hair, blue eyes, and six-foot-one stature, I became utterly Chinese. In either case—if I was seen as Taiwanese or Chinese—my father wanted me to understand that my identity and actions would be interpreted as an act of betraying Chinese solidarity.

I told my father that how the Chinese would feel about me could not intimidate me into not going to the mainland. The other and, I thought, greater source of my parents' concern about my trip was that they did not know what to make of my relationship with Billy. My parents and I shared extremely different sets of emotional vocabularies for relationships. Our differences were both generational and cultural. For them, two people were either friends, or they were husband and wife. Very little existed in between. In their case, neither of them had dated anyone else, so it was even more difficult for them to imagine all the possibilities that can and did exist in between. Instead of describing these possibilities to them, I reverted to my parents' set of oversimplified descriptions and assured them that Billy and I were "just friends," when in fact, we had been dating for a year and a half.

My parents were not going to tell me directly that I could not go to China, just as they were never going to tell me to my face that they wanted me to become a Taiwanese citizen. But they pressed on with the different reasons why I was not ready to take this trip. My mother finally made me feel as though going to China would be something terrible I was doing to her. She was vague about how this might be true, but it was typical of her to end any discussion with the last word: "Well, do what you want, but know that this whole thing makes me very uncomfortable."

We were on the phone after she and my father had returned to Taiwan, and she promptly hung up, leaving me dangling and writhing with an undeserved feeling of guilt. This tactic was not uncommon for her. She used to call me from Taiwan on her birthday and say, "Hello. It's your mother. I just wanted to tell you not to bother calling anymore. We're twelve hours ahead of you here, and my birthday is practically over."

So my brother offered me this advice: Weigh the guilt you will feel if you go to China against the disappointment you will feel if you don't go, and then you will know what to do. What he meant was: The guilt will always outweigh the disappointment—don't go.

Only my father asked me why I wanted to go to China. The rest of us—myself included—didn't bother asking because the answer seemed too obvious. "Because I've never been there," was my reply. Now I see how that was too easy, too careless. My family didn't support my going to China with Billy, but I didn't give them enough reason to understand my wanting to go with Billy, either. I wasn't going to change my mind about the trip, but it did feel strange—almost wrong—to go on a trip that my family didn't approve.

Then something happened to change the circumstances of my trip. My father later told us that throughout our reunion in Monterey, he had been having a series of nightmares. In the middle of the night, he would startle himself awake because his heart would be beating so fast and hard in his chest that he would have to grasp for air. He never remembered what the nightmares were about, only that he woke up feeling so nervous that he could not breathe. It happened again on the plane ride back to Taiwan after our reunion. Everyone else in the cabin was asleep, including my mother. Her head had been resting on my father's chest, and she half opened her eyes when she felt him jerk suddenly. She put her hand limply over my father's, rolled her head the other way, and fell back asleep. The nightmare had made him feel so bad this time that my father considered waking my mother to tell her. He wanted her to put her hand on his chest and feel how desperately his heart was beating. But he hated to worry her, and he had a golf date with a friend when they arrived in Taipei in the morning. He would tell her after golf, my father decided.

It turned out that the series of nightmares my father was having was a series of angina attacks—overtightening of his heart muscles because of clogged arteries—each one threatening to crescendo to full blast. My father later said that he had never been taught to talk about his feelings, so he did not know how to even begin describing how these angina attacks felt. The most accurate description he could find, then, was that they felt as if he were caught in the terrible web of a nightmare.

A family friend, Dr. Sung, was a cardiologist at Stanford Hospital, and he insisted that my father fly to Stanford for all his procedures. He told my father that if he needed open-heart surgery, there were far fewer risks in the

United States than in Taiwan. When my parents arrived in California for what they hoped would just be a few tests, they brought two large suitcases and moved into the guest room in my Uncle Jack's house in San Mateo. I packed my bags, left my apartment in San Francisco, and moved into my cousin Margie's empty bedroom. My brother, Alex, was scheduled to fly into San Francisco from Hong Kong in a few days. Time seemed to stand still— everything outside of my father's heart filtered out of our lives. Everything became periphery and faded out of focus. As a family, we were strangely alert and prepared for this. Fifteen years ago, we had skipped my father's fortieth birthday because a fortune-teller once warned that my father might die of a heart attack as suddenly as my grandfather had when he was forty. My father was forty-one two years in a row. He didn't have a heart attack then. Instead, my father became diabetic, which put him at an even higher risk for heart disease.

The first procedure the doctors performed on my father was an angiogram, which took a photograph of my father's heart. Only my mother was with him when Dr. Sung showed them my father's heart. I imagine my mother grabbing my father's hand when the doctor used his pointer to tap three times on the large blue and gray negative to show where three of his arteries were more than eighty percent clogged. Dr. Sung told my parents it was a miracle my father was still alive.

We had to wait a month for my father's surgery. That was the earliest the heart surgeon could operate on my father. We tried to keep busy while we waited anxiously. We watched movies; ate at different restaurants; visited my uncles, aunts, and my grandmother on my mother's side. Meiguo Ah-ma had moved into Uncle Jack's house, as well. We rarely talked about how afraid we were. The challenge was to make it to the surgery date in February without losing control. So we talked about other things. One night, after Alex had flown in from Hong Kong, the four of us gathered on the bed in my parents' makeshift bedroom. My father was lying under the covers, and the rest of us were sitting around the bed, encircling him.

"Xiao bao," my father said.

"Yeah, Daddy?"

"Tell us about Billy," he said. His voice was tender, his tone earnest. I could feel myself stiffen. We were never taught how to speak openly about our feelings with our parents. Most of what my family understood of each other was inferred from our actions. Otherwise, we wrote our feelings in letters. But even writing limited my ability to relay my deeper feelings with my parents, as all my letters to them have always been written in Chinese (and many of them would be mailed back to me with wrong characters circled in red and rewritten correctly on the backside in my mother's handwriting). I have a much greater command of my emotions in English than I do in Chinese. The question seemed too basic to be asked of someone with whom I already had such a profound relationship. But the truth was, my parents didn't know anything about Billy because I had kept quiet about him, relishing my privacy and freedom to live my life without having to report back to my parents. So I started from the beginning.

We had met the summer of 1997 in St. Petersburg, Russia. We were on the same study-abroad program. Billy was studying political science—mainly Soviet politics—at Berkeley, and I was doing a minor in Russian literature at Vassar. The first month we were in St. Petersburg, we got to know each other in that accelerated pace which happens when you meet someone while traveling. It hardly mattered how little we knew of one another's past and what would happen when summer was over. For the time being, we were suspended in the magical haze of St. Petersburg's "white nights," when the sun didn't set for two whole months. It felt as though we were awake for the first time—we were so conscious of something extraordinary happening for us. We had just met, but already there was so little we had to explain to each other because there was so much we understood.

A month into the program, my father had called to tell me that Ah-gong, the grandfather who had given me my Chinese name, had died from a stroke. I was the only one in my family who did not go to the funeral. Everyone agreed that Ah-gong would have wanted me to finish my studies in Russia. When the three Russian women I lived with—Babushka Sema; her daughter, Nina; and Nina's daughter, Larissa—saw that I had been crying all afternoon, they wrapped their arms around me, shushing me, kissing me, calling me Solnitsa, Brendochka—"little sunshine," "little Brenda." Russian words of comfort gushed out from their lips, and I blinked back at them, unable to answer. I was unready to call up the words to communicate my sorrow in English or in Chinese, and much less in Russian. In a daze, I excused myself and walked fifteen minutes to Billy's apartment.

When he opened the door, I simply told him, "My grandfather died." He pulled me into his room and held me tightly, smoothing my hair with his hand, kissing the top of my head. We were silent for what seemed a long time. He had understood that was what I needed from him. Finally, I said, "Tell me a story," and he told me a story from Russian history. Later, I fell asleep on his bed, my eyes tired from crying. I slept on my stomach with my hand curled up by my face, the way my mother told me I had liked to fall asleep when I was a baby. Billy sat beside me, his hand gently rubbing small circles on my back.

By the end of the summer, what was so magical about our two months in St. Petersburg was our conviction that this was only the beginning of something we would share for a long time. At the time, we could not articulate what, exactly, had happened because the feeling was still so fresh and new and real. All we knew was that we had each other now and that somehow the world made more sense because of it.

When I was back at school, I called my mother and tried to tell her what had happened to me over the summer. My end of the conversation became awkward when I realized she did not understand or was not ready to accept what I was trying to say. I had begun to tell her but soon felt embarrassed for suddenly being so candid with my mother about matters of the heart. It's not something we had ever shared with each other.

But now, in the week before my father's open-heart surgery, my father was asking me to open up to him. He genuinely wanted to know. His eyes were closed as he listened to me talk. I could feel my mother watching me intently in my periphery, but really, it was my father with whom I was communicating. I knew he understood, even as I described Billy in such abstract and emotionally charged terms. Once, my father had written to me about the time he realized he had begun to fall in love with my mother. Rereading his letter, I realized how we are alike in the way we are unable to find precise adjectives to describe being in love. It is a feeling so much larger than ourselves that descriptions feel inadequate, and we both tend to relate feeling love for an individual with how we feel about the world at large. "Our meeting," he had written about my mother, "was full of feeling. Since then, I began seeing Mommy in a different light—I still do, today . . . She is the only one who has opened my eyes to so many different things in the world."

I have never seen my father look as small and vulnerable as on the day of his heart surgery. The surgeons let us go see him a few minutes before he would be pushed into the surgery room. My father's hand was cold and tired. The anesthesia was already taking effect. His eyes were heavy with sleep. I leaned over my father and kissed him on his forehead. "Don't be afraid," I whispered.

"I'm not," he said drowsily. Two doctors swung back the curtains to wheel his gurney out. I saw my mother squeeze my father's leg.

"See you soon, Daddy!" My mother waved at my father as he was pushed out of the curtained area. She bit her bottom lip. When he was almost at the double swinging doors, my father managed to raise his right hand limply. He waved, his fingers curled into his palm.

Open heart, translated literally into Mandarin is kai xin—it means "happy." After his surgery, my father began calling this operation his kai xin surgery, his happy surgery. The head surgeon told my father that his life had just been extended for another twenty, maybe thirty, years. It was hardly the first thing my father said to me after his surgery, but before he and my mother flew back to Taiwan in early March, he held me close and said to me, "I want you to go to China, Xiao bao. I am so happy you are going to China."

NATIONALITY

When I think back on our first trip to China, it feels as though Billy and I were always on the train, headed somewhere but never quite getting there. Most of my memories of that trip are accompanied by the rhythmic clacking of the train on its tracks, the rush of Chinese landscape outside our slightly opened windows, and the warm breeze brushing against our cheeks. We were always on the train. We slept in open coupes with other travelers. We played cards with our bunkmates and made friends with our neighbors. Billy listened to Mandarin cassette tapes on his Walkman while following the lessons in his language exercise book. I drew cartoons and wrote in my journal, and we played countless games of Mastermind and Hangman. All of this while on our way to some destination in China, where it felt as though the train sighed, stopped momentarily at the station, and then moved on again. I once read a strange Russian novella about a group of people on a train traveling toward a broken bridge, only they never get to the bridge, and the people on the train became a community of perpetual travelers—together in their rootlessness with the blur of never-ending train tracks whooshing past underneath. That was how our time in China felt to me even though we had stopped in ten different cities along the east coast from Hong Kong to Beijing over a period of thirty days, which was the longest our Chinese visas would allow us to stay on the mainland.

It wasn't that the ten cities we visited were unmemorable. On the contrary, I was ceaselessly moved by the diversity of the Chinese landscape the farther north—and sometimes inland—we traveled, and though my eyes were accustomed to the typical colors and styles of Chinese architecture that were prevalent in Taiwan, I still found myself marveling at the poetic, detailed construction of old and new buildings in both larger cities and smaller towns. It was, after all, my first time on the mainland. Everything I saw, I drank in excitedly, greedily. What draws my memories of China to our train rides has, I've decided, to do with the sense of community and mutuality I shared with the other Chinese travelers. While on the train, we were between places, neither here nor there yet. And in this shared state of transition, people tended to be less judgmental about, and more interested in, where I was from and where Billy and I were going. We were all of us travelers; we shared a similar identity. I noticed that the Chinese people we met when we were not on a train were less sympathetic toward me—they were more possessive of their Chineseness and their homeland and consequently became guarded against my Taiwanese- and Americanness.

That my being Taiwanese would be offensive to a Chinese person was something I had already experienced before going to China. During my last year of college, I had shared a townhouse with three other women. One of them, Anna, had been born in Shanghai, and her family had moved to New York when she was twelve. She and I both worked as Mandarin drill instructors in the Chinese department. Another one of our housemates, Melissa, had been born in Queens after her parents had emigrated from Taiwan to New York during Taiwan's brain drain. At home, Melissa's parents spoke to her in Taiwanese. Often, she and I would mix in a few Taiwanese phrases with our English. Once, Anna overheard us and stomped angrily toward us.

"Look," she said sternly, pushing her face close to mine. She stuck out her thumb. "This is Mainland China." She bent her thumb down and now raised her little pinky, wriggling it around, and said in a mocking, high voice, "And this is Taiwan." She looked back and forth between me and Melissa, opening her eyes wide. "We are going to swallow you up. You hear? Swallow. You. Up."

I remember I laughed as if Anna had just told us a funny joke. But when we each returned to our separate rooms, I thought to myself how she must have been echoing something she had heard her parents say at home. I could almost see her father pounding the dinner table one night and hear the violence in his voice when he described the way he wanted China to reclaim this insolent, rebel island. Even though I had never met him, I could hear traces of his voice in Anna's, because whether our generation feels Taiwan should be reunified with China or be granted full independence, we largely base our opinions on the way our parents feel. The issue is more complex than mere politics—it is about family and history, nationality and Chinese solidarity.

In China, I found I was intimidated by the Chinese. Of course part of this was because my one exchange with Anna and my father's forewarnings had made me feel that I should be cautious around the Chinese. The other part of my intimidation was borne out of (mis)interpreting the way certain people looked at me and the way they pressed me to tell them the specificities of my family background. I relied on the Chinese to show me how much they wanted to accept me as Taiwanese. And American. And Chinese. Sometimes I believed that it would be better if I lied and told people that my parents had emigrated to the United States and that I had grown up there, and not in Taiwan. I would appear less harmful if I were more American than Taiwanese. The first time I told this lie was when we were in Shaoshan— Mao's birthplace—and Billy and I were talking to two khaki-uniformed soldiers who were on a break from marching and goose-stepping around the grounds surrounding a gigantic bronze statue of Mao. There was an entire army there that day, it seemed. As I eyed the soldiers' steel-toed boots and gleaming rifles, the lie rolled off my tongue easily, persuasively. Out of the corner of my eye, I could see Billy looking at me; he was amused by this editing and reconstructing of my background. When the soldiers learned that I had "grown up in America," the first question they asked me was whether I had been to Chinatown. I looked into their faces and found expectant smiles, the kind of smiles one might find on children who have never been to Disneyland and want to know whether it really is a wonderland with life-size cartoon characters and rides that go through dark tunnels and shoot you back out into the daylight.

When we walked around the streets in China—and especially when Billy and I were in smaller towns—I always felt self-conscious because of the way people unabashedly stared at us. It was strange how the children were more easily embarrassed than the adults. Men and women looked at us without any qualms, making me uneasy, while children were less obvious— and gentler—about their curiosity.

On one of our first nights in China, in a city called Changsha, Billy and I sat down on some steps outside our hotel after dinner, making plans for the following day. Two little girls—about eight years old—sat on tiny portable wicker chairs behind two small baskets that held shoe-shining tools. They occupied the space about ten feet away from where Billy and I were sitting. As soon as they spotted us, they whispered excitedly to each other, giggling hysterically after each exchange of secrets. They were not wanting to shine our shoes, as Billy and I were both wearing canvas sneakers. One girl seemed to be more reserved than the other, more boisterous and bossy girl. When Billy would talk to me and his head turned away from the girls, I noticed that they would grab their seats with one hand and their baskets with the other and scurry a few steps closer to us. As soon as Billy turned his head in their direction, they would clumsily set their chairs back down and sit on them and kick their skinny little legs up as if they had been sitting there idly for some time. Billy and I played this silent game with them for a while until they had arrived directly in front of us, and the four of us sat across from each other, laughing at and with each other. We made friends quickly—Billy and I appreciated their girlish playfulness, and they appreciated our not exposing their ploy to get as close to us as possible.

The adults did not seem as kind or simply curious. As we walked past vendors squatting on the sidewalks, intermittently smoking cigarettes and turning their heads to spit, they never failed to stop what they were doing to look from Billy to me and back to Billy again, trying to figure us out. Growing up, I had been used to being stared at. The Chinese school children had all worn navy blue uniforms with yellow canvas hats that had an elastic band connected to them, which snapped under their chins. Boys had to have their hair in crew cuts, while girls were not allowed to let their hair grow past their ears. My classmates and I, however, had worn whatever we wanted to school, and the girls all had long hair, which we swished from left to right proudly against our backs when we bounced down the streets. People had stared. They had known we were different from other kids, and I didn't mind the attention. Then, I prided myself in being different—being, specifically, American. But in China, I wanted to be left alone. I missed my anonymity and wished at times that I could be invisible.

There were times when I envied Billy his limited Mandarin. When he didn't feel like communicating with people on the streets—mostly vendors and taxi drivers soliciting business—he didn't have to. He could "turn off" his ear to anything spoken in Chinese and let it all fade into a cacophony of unintelligible sounds. He could, in his utter contrast in physical appearance to Chinese people, become invisible. And when he did turn around to surprise a vendor with a few words of Mandarin, he would be slapped on the back with a smile that bespoke such genuine approval and liking that I could not help feeling jealous. I, on the other hand, could not pretend I didn't understand Chinese. I could not pretend I wasn't, in some small way, Chinese. I became, in my undeniably Chinese physical appearance—with my slight stature, brown eyes, black hair, and round face—utterly, and sometimes painfully, visible.

Once, I tried to pretend I could not understand that a rickshaw peddler was trying to get Billy and me to take a ride around the city with him. We walked by. Billy smiled politely at him. I completely ignored him, "turning off" my ears while hearing and understanding every word that was being said. The peddler wanted this much for a half-hour ride. All right, all right, he would lower the price a little. Okay? Okay? How about it? I looked straight ahead. When we were about ten feet away, the peddler yelled loudly down the street, "What! Have you forgotten your Chinese? Do you not know how to speak a word of it?" I heard other people laughing behind me, goading the rickshaw peddler. Yeah, yeah, she doesn't understand a word of it! Haha. "Huh!" he continued yelling. "You! Who do you think you are anyway? You are a wai guo ren!" I winced.

Literally, "wai guo ren" means a "person (ren) from outside (wai) the country (guo)," or foreigner. One is either Chinese or wai guo ren. You cannot be both. For the Middle Kingdom, everyone else was peripheral, because Chinese solidarity has always been built upon the basis of exclusion and, consequently, seclusion. In China, one's identity is either/or—you are either inside, or you are outside. I was both, and people were not sure what to make of me. Extremes were much easier to understand and accept than all the possibilities that existed in between. How Chinese was I? How Taiwanese? Did I threaten to worsen the Chinese diaspora? Chinese descriptions are often hyperbolic and have to be qualified with adjectives such as very or most. A girl is always "very pretty" or "most pretty;" she is never just "pretty." Words like very and most work like the verb to be in English so that descriptions are always extreme. This is another reason why I think I posed a bit of a problem for the Chinese—I was not very Chinese (because I was more Taiwanese), nor was I very American (the way Billy clearly was), nor was I very Taiwanese (because I was also a little American and a little Chinese), and I really wasn't even very foreign, because I spoke Chinese fluently and was accustomed to most of the Chinese cultural nuances that I had grown up with in Taiwan. Sometimes I think it might have been easier on all of us if I hadn't understood or spoken Chinese at all. Then I could just be the wai guo ren that the rickshaw peddler had accused me of being.

When we were in Qufu, the town where Confucius was born, Billy and I ran into some trouble trying to get a hotel room. From the train station, we had boarded a minibus taxi packed full of people—Billy had to stand some of the way with his head pushed up at an angle against the ceiling of the car—making several stops depositing the passengers until it was just Billy and me and the driver. Looking out the window, I saw that the streets were empty and all the shops looked closed. Signs were rusted, and some even swung precariously off their signposts. The branches on the trees along the street had been pruned to blunt stumps. I noticed the bus driver looking at us in his rearview mirror. When he caught my eye in the mirror, he rolled his eyes away, used his index finger and thumb to take the cigarette that was dangling from his bottom lip and throw it—angrily, I thought—out the window. When we arrived at our hotel, the driver got out of the car with us and walked ahead of us into the lobby, his hips thrust out in a gait that made it look as though he owned the hotel. He slapped the counter of the front desk three times with his palm before he put his elbows on the countertop and leaned over. A receptionist who had been bent over, studying her nails, looked up at the driver. He took the soft pack of cigarettes from the breast pocket of his shirt and flicked his head in our direction. With a quick flip of his wrist, a solitary cigarette rose out of the small, square opening of the pack like a little soldier standing at attention.

The receptionist studied us for a while before she bowed her head again, this time to open a folder and flip through its plastic sleeves.

"Two rooms?" she asked me, her voice muffled against her chest.

"Just one," I said.

She looked up. "I'll need your marriage certificate, then."

The driver suddenly choked on his cigarette and coughed, "You two are married?"

I turned to Billy and said to him in English. "They want a marriage certificate. What are we supposed to do?" He looked at me and blinked. Then he slapped his forehead with the palm of his hand and said, melodramatically, startling all of us, "I left it at home!"

"They *are* married!" The driver buried his head in his hands, his cigarette burning dangerously close to his scalp. "I just can't believe this. A Chinese girl and a foreigner. Can you believe this?" he asked the receptionist. Then he went on and on, mumbling and shaking his head, looking at me disdainfully. I suspect that had I not spoken any Chinese, I would have been as much a foreigner as Billy was and the driver would not have looked at me as though I had betrayed our race.

Many people in China had difficulty accepting my relationship with Billy. In cities like Beijing and Shanghai, of course, this was less so than in smaller cities like Datong. Datong was a lonely, deserted mining town that was home to Buddhist caves dating back to the fifth century. Billy and I took the train eight hours inland from Beijing to see these Buddhist caves. Once there, we had to take a bus to get to the caves. All along the streets, through the thin veil of black soot blown from the mines, we saw sheets and clothes hanging outside apartment windows. The clothes fluttered in the wind, looking like ghosts in a forgotten town. We waited by the roadside for a long while for our bus. A man came and joined us, and though he stood a few feet away, I could feel his eyes darting back and forth between Billy and me. By that time in our trip, we had gotten used to ignoring the stares. Sometimes people were genuinely curious; at other times their eyes betrayed a look of judgment, the way the driver in Qufu had made me feel I should be ashamed of myself. This man at the bus stop was just curious. I knew because of the way he seemed to be straining to hear our exchange of English words. He was looking at us, but he was looking to hear us better. Then I heard him clear his throat, and I turned toward him.

"So how much money do you make?" he blurted.

"What?" I gasped, unable to believe what this man had surmised about my relationship to Billy.

"How much do you make? I hear you make a lot of money in your business." He nodded at me and, I thought, looked at me hungrily. Then he suddenly turned to walk away—he had not been waiting for the bus after all. As he walked away, I watched him stick his hands in his pockets and heard him mutter under his breath, "Yeah, you translators make a lot of money."

The wonderful thing about our train rides was that there, Billy and I could be travelers just like everyone else. We were a part of a collective, and I found that being among that particular crowd gave me more freedom to be an observer. An especially memorable train ride was our fifteen-hour trip from Changsha to Hangzhou. Those fifteen hours felt like an accelerated lifetime in miniature in which people came in and out of our lives as they came on and off the train at the intermediary stops. The interior of the train soon became a familiar space. For fifteen hours, the train was our home.

The Chinese passenger train system is separated into four categories: hard seats, soft seats, hard sleepers, and soft sleepers. Sleepers are generally for overnight train rides, and the seats for day trips. Hard sleepers work this way: on one side of the train are open compartments of six bunks, and on the other side of the train is a narrow walkway. Underneath each window on that side of the train are tabletops and two fold-out seats that face each other. Each bunk is equipped with a thin white mattress, a flimsy pillow, and a wool blanket folded neatly at one end of the bunk. My father would have said that the blankets were folded like cakes of dried, soy-sauce tofu. During his service in the army, he told me, that was how they were taught to make their beds. No matter which bunk you were on, there was very limited head room, so the foldout seats by the windows were highly coveted seats during the hours when most people were awake.

This was supposed to be an air-conditioned train, but it was hot and stuffy. The air was stagnant and smelled of perspiring bodies. At first, we thought that the air had not been turned on because the train had not yet started to move, but the rumor was that the air conditioner had broken down. All around, men had stripped down to their undershirts and were fanning themselves with anything they could find to create some kind of a breeze. When the train finally jerked to a start, the air coming in through the windows provided some relief.

In the open coupe next to ours, a man was sitting in his sleeveless undershirt that exposed his skinny arms as he lit a cigarette and grumbled angrily under his breath. On the bed across from him sat an overweight man in his early thirties, his face glistening with sweat and oil as he huffed and puffed heavily, short of breath. He had eyes that were round and kind, a face that resembled a child's.

"Hey," he said timidly to the skinny man, "you're not allowed to smoke in the cars. You should go between cars for that." Then he lowered his head quickly and concentrated on opening a package of cookies, hoping that he had not insulted his bunkmate.

The skinny man, sitting hunched over, took one long drag of his cigarette and then exhaled dramatically. "Huh!" he scoffed, smoke still coming out of his mouth. "What do I care about these rules? I paid for an air-conditioned train ride, and if this is what I get, I'm just going to smoke wherever the hell I please." He looked at the fat man, who had successfully opened his pack of cookies and was happily shoving them into his mouth, already in another world and not caring whether his bunkmate was breaking the rules. The skinny man stuck his cigarette in his mouth and left it sticking to his bottom lip. He peered at the fat man and then stuck out his hand, holding his pack of cigarettes.

The fat man looked up, cookie crumbs stuck to his face. He shook his head vigorously. "Oh no," he said with his mouth full, somewhat horrified. "I'll go in between cars when I need one."

"Oh come on . . . don't be such a wimp. Nobody cares. We deserve at least this much—the freedom to smoke wherever we choose!" The skinny man laughed through pursed lips. When he laughed, the ashes at the end of his burning cigarette fluttered slowly to the floor.

I sat under one of the windows, across from Billy, and watched the two men interact. There was something comical about the whole scene. Perhaps it seemed almost theatrical to me because I could observe them from my seat, unnoticed. Over the PA system, a woman dj was introducing the music that blared from the invisible speakers in our car. With melodramatic intonations, she announced that the next song would be a dedication from a young man in car number six to the young lady in car number seven.

All down our car, people were talking loudly and excitedly. It was as if all in our car had known one other for many years and were taking a trip out of town together. Two coupes down, six people were sitting on the two lower bunks, playing a card game. The skinny man and fat man duo had engaged in a conversation that went beyond the skinny man intimidating the fat man into smoking in the car. Every seat under the windows was taken by men who drank tea from recycled glass jars with soggy tea leaves swimming sleepily at the bottom. Most of the women travelers had already climbed onto their assigned bunks and turned toward the wall to turn in for the night, although somewhere about three coupes' distance, I heard the whispers and reserved giggles of young women.

Sitting behind Billy was a small, thin man whose face was half covered with his oversized plastic glasses. He had turned sideways in his seat, I suspected, so that he could listen to our conversation. We had been discussing why there were so many Chinese travelers everywhere we went. Billy, who had started studying Chinese history after we had met that summer in Russia, explained that it was because Mao had encouraged domestic travel—it was a way to build solidarity, because one must understand one's own country to have national pride. Furthermore, travel for Chinese people outside the mainland was nearly impossible; where else could people go?

At this point, the man sitting behind Billy leaned over and tapped him on the shoulder.

"Excuse me?" he said in English.

Billy swiveled around. "Hey," he said, as if he and the man behind him already knew each other.

"Yes. I am wondering . . . ah . . . I was interested in knowing why you are traveling in China?" He had a slight Chinese accent, but we were already impressed with his English. He cocked his small, triangular head to one side and blinked his eyes a few times behind those big glasses.

"Well," Billy began, looking back at me, "we wanted to see it. We've never been here before." He turned back to look at the man. "We're tourists," he added.

"Ah, I see." He pushed his glasses up with his index finger and then let out an embarrassed laugh. He stuck out his thin hand at Billy. "I'm Perseus."

"I'm Billy." They shook hands. "Perseus, huh? Where'd you get a name like Perseus? It's pretty original," Billy complimented.

Perseus pushed his glasses up again and closed his eyes briefly in a moment of pride.

"You like it? I named myself! Do you know the story about Perseus? He was the hero who killed that monster . . . what was the name . . . ah! Medusa! Very smart fellow. And then he married a very beautiful girl." He paused and chuckled. "Maybe one day I will marry a beautiful girl, too." I learned later that he had named himself Perseus because his Chinese name was Ying Xiong, which means "hero." He leaned into the aisle to try to get a glimpse of me. He motioned in my direction. "Your friend?"

"Uh . . . yeah. Bren, come over." I walked over and stood next to Billy, taking up the rest of the space in the narrow walkway. "This is Perseus."

"Hi," I said, not sure whether I should use Chinese or English. "I'm Brenda."

"You are Chinese?"

I looked at Billy. "I'm American," I blurted.

"What do you mean?"

"I was born in America." I looked at his puzzled face and felt sorry that I had caused it to scrunch up like that. "But yeah, I'm Chinese."

"And your parents? They were born in China?"

I switched to Mandarin. "Actually, they were born in Taiwan. They still live there." I searched Perseus' face to see whether my being from Taiwan bothered him.

Perseus spoke back to me in Chinese, too. His tone changed—it was softer, more understanding. "Oh, I see, but you were sent to America for your schooling."

"Right."

"And you and your friend are traveling together?"

"Yeah."

I could tell he still had a lot of questions to ask me, but he turned his attention back to Billy and began speaking in his careful, measured English. I was relieved and remained more or less silent by Billy's side. I thought interjecting Chinese might disrupt the flow of their conversation, and then I was afraid that if I joined in with English, Perseus might think me snobbish, showing off my English. We learned that Perseus was studying economics at the university in Shanghai and that he had never left the mainland. He told us it was too difficult to get a visa to leave the country. We were even more impressed with his English—he spoke with only a few of the odd phrases that one learns from language textbooks that end up being not very colloquial at all. When Billy used phrases he'd learned from his Mandarin workbook, for example, I often had to tell him that no one uses those phrases in everyday speech anymore.

"Will you be traveling to Beijing?" Perseus asked.

"It will be our last stop," Billy explained.

Perseus considered this. He looked up, his eyebrows furrowed, "Maybe this is not a good time to see Beijing. Many parts of the city—like Tiananmen Square—have been closed for renovation." He saw that we were surprised. "In October, there will be a big celebration for the fiftieth anniversary of China." He meant the fiftieth anniversary of Communist China.

Billy asked Perseus what else he thought was going to be closed when a sudden outburst of girlish laughter interrupted their conversation. Perseus turned around to look behind him. Four women in their early twenties were sitting on the bottom two bunks of their coupe, looking over at us.

"Eh!" one of them called out to Perseus. "You know that wai guo ren?"

"No," Perseus smiled. "We just met."

"Then can you ask him to come over and talk to us? We want to practice our English." The girl who was talking was big-boned, wearing a button-down denim shirt tucked into dark blue denim pants that tapered at her ankles. The girl who sat next to her was skinny and had her hand on her friend's thigh. I noticed that she was intermittently pinching and slapping her friend's thigh, covering her mouth with her other hand as she giggled bashfully.

"You're not really asking him to come over here, are you?" She whispered loudly to her friend. She was so excited.

"Of course I am! You wanted me to do it! Now stop pinching me!" She spoke Mandarin with a Beijing accent—the *er* sounds were rolled dramatically, *sh* sounds made with deliberate emphasis. We learned later that the girls were not from Beijing but that the "proper" way to speak Mandarin is always with a Beijing—the "official"—accent; in a sense, it was like the way all the time zones spread across the expanse of China were "consolidated" to adhere to one time zone—Beijing's. The girl looked at Billy and nodded her head. "H-he-hello," she said in English.

"What are you girls so shy about?" Perseus called. "If you want to practice your English, you can't be shy. Just look at me!" He smiled widely, his little cheeks pushing up his glasses.

"Exactly," the big-boned girl said and glared at her friend.

Perseus turned to Billy and said, "Those ladies there were wondering if you would help them with their English. They want to talk with you."

Billy looked up at me. I shrugged my shoulders. "Let's go," I said. We walked over to the girls' coupe. Perseus stayed in his seat, where he was close enough to hear the conversation. As we were standing next to their bunks, someone from the adjacent coupe—the group playing cards—stuck her hand out and touched my arm. She tugged on my sleeve.

"Come and play," she invited. She spoke Chinese with a different accent, one that I could not place. I left Billy with the girls and ducked behind a leg hanging from a top bunk to take a seat next to the girl who had asked me to play cards. The group immediately broke into a dialect I had never heard before. I could make out some words, but couldn't make sense of anything. I asked them what dialect they were speaking.

"We're from Changsha, Hunan Province," a man from the top bunk answered.

On another train the day before, Billy and I had sat across from a young man from Zhuzhou, which is also in Hunan Province. He was very curious about America and even more curious about Billy. He didn't speak a word of English and so spoke slowly in Mandarin to Billy. When Billy couldn't understand, the man looked to me for translation. He confirmed that America was split up into states and then asked whether Americans spoke different dialects of English from state to state. Billy told him no—that people spoke with different accents, but not in different dialects—and the man from Zhuzhou was surprised. "So everyone speaks the exact same language all the time?" Billy and I nodded. Our friend explained to us that in China, there were countless dialects even though Mandarin was the official national language taught in schools. I had known that but hadn't been aware that even within a province, people from different cities speak different dialects. The people playing cards spoke a specific Changsha dialect. I asked, in Mandarin, for them to teach me something in Changsha.

"All right. For instance," the woman who sat next to me said, "what would you usually say to someone when he is leaving your house?"

"Good-bye—zai jian?" I offered.

"No, no." She laughed softly, putting her hand gently on mine. "More polite."

"Oh! Then, man zou," I tried again. That means "walk slowly."

"Right," she said. "Sometimes, we even say hao zou—"walk well"—right?" I nodded. "Well, in Changsha, it's the same thing, except you pronounce it huh zeh." She pushed her chin out as she demonstrated for me. I repeated it silently.

"Try it! Say it out loud!" the man from the opposite top bunk encouraged.

"Huh zeh," I tried slowly. And then I repeated it, louder. "Huh zeh." Everyone laughed. The woman sitting next to me squeezed my hand.

"Close!" "Not bad!" "That's right!" Approvals shot out from all sides of the coupe. At that moment I felt, as Billy must have felt whenever he was praised for his Mandarin, a sense of their eager acceptance of me. It was a short moment, but it was one of the few times in China when I had felt genuinely comfortable and at ease.

Later, I joined Billy in his coupe, where he was surrounded by the four giggling university girls. The big-boned girl, who seemed to be the least shy among her classmates, asked me in Mandarin how to say certain words. She wanted to ask Billy questions about NATO and Hillary Clinton. She then asked if I was sure that it would not be too "sensitive" to talk so candidly about politics; I assured her that she could ask whatever she wanted, that she did not need to be afraid or too cautious. She practiced her new vocabulary words with me a few times as her friends watched with excitement and admiration.

She took a deep breath and prepared herself, pushing the palms of her hands down the front of her jeans nervously. "Okay," she said. Now she held her breath and closed her eyes briefly before looking straight at Billy.

"Can you," she began in English, "can you tell me how you feel . . . " Her friends and I waited expectantly, we were hardly breathing ourselves. And then she gushed in one long, connected word, "Canyoutellmehowyoufeel-aboutChowYunFat?" She let out her breath.

We all had a good laugh.

Then it was Billy's turn to ask the girls about politics. He asked the girls how they felt about Jiang Zemin, the president of China. The same girl who had tried to ask about NATO answered for the rest of them. Her answer sounded well rehearsed.

"We like Jiang Zemin," she declared. "We think he is the father of China."

Of course, I thought, these girls were ready to attribute all of China's successes and pitfalls to one man. From dynastic emperors to Mao Zedong, power in China has always been absolute and centralized. People needed to believe in a figure—a father figure—who provided unquestioned power and benevolent guidance. Distribution of power within the government was still a relatively new concept.

Later on the same train ride, while Billy was sleeping on a top bunk, I sat down under a window to write in my journal. Two men wearing old wool sport jackets approached me and said that they had overheard some of our conversations from earlier. They asked me about America ("We hear there's not a single speck of dust there because it is so clean!") and then about Taiwan ("Is it true that everyone in Taiwan is rich?"). One man leaned against the side of the train, looked around him, and sighed, shaking his head slowly before saying, "If Chiang Kai-shek had won the war back in 1949, maybe we could be as well off as Taiwan is now!" He and his friend laughed. Their laughter was nervous, but also a little sad. I wondered about their rumination. What would have happened if Chiang had won the war against Mao? I don't know. I did know that Taiwan was "well off," as they'd put it, because of many different factors—the Japanese occupation; Chiang Kai-shek's authoritarian leadership; and now, a budding, full-democratic government in which power was well-distributed within a system of checks and balances modeled largely after the United States' government. And maybe Taiwan's successes were also due, in large part, to its small, contained, and manageable size.

When we arrived in Beijing, only Tiananmen Square was completely closed off. Everything else was under heavy construction. Bamboo scaffolding latticework masked building and monument facades. Fortunately, we were still able to visit Mao's mausoleum and the Imperial Palace. It was on our tour of the Imperial Palace (the "Forbidden City") that I learned more about the Chinese concept of power.

To enter the Imperial Palace, we had to walk through the central tunnel of the Meridian Gate. Inside, it was dark and cool and a little moist. Our voices bounced off the walls and whispered back to us. When we came out of the other end of the tunnel and were met by the light and sudden expanse of the outer court, I felt as though I had been sent back in time. The other side of the tunnel—where Beijing streets bustled with cars and bicycles—seemed ages ago. We were looking at a scalloped ochre roof supported by red pillars. The same structures surrounded us on all sides. From where we stood, the second gate was a five-minute walk away. Two stone lions guarded the gate—the one on the right is always the female, who has a baby lion under her left paw; and the lion on the left is the male, who controls the world under his right paw.

The woman at the ticket office had given us a map of the palace. On the cover, there was an aerial photograph of the entire Forbidden City. Seen from that perspective, I suddenly understood the architectural design. At first glance, the palace looked like a labyrinth—wall after wall, corner bent around corner. But when I held the photograph at arm's length and squinted my eyes at it—the way I would when looking at an Impressionist painting from afar—what surfaced was an image of a robe. The shape was roughly a T, as if the robe were being hung for presentation with outstretched arms. The layout of the palace appeared to correspond to parts of the human body. The farther inward we walked, the closer we got to the "neck" of the robe (the head of the body), where the Son of Heaven, the Emperor, would have sat to rule the Middle Kingdom.

The Emperor had almost never left the Forbidden City. He was protected and imprisoned within the walls of the Imperial Palace. A Chinese emperor lived in a world that had little to do with his country. He did not go out into the country to see how his people lived. He did not go out into the country to understand what his people's problems might be. From his world of concubines and servants—a world where he was revered as a direct descendant of the most mythical and auspicious of animals, the Dragon—he ruled all of China. He made all the decisions. His power was absolute. But it was so also because the Chinese had a deep trust for their emperors, their leaders. Sometimes, respect and blind devotion became synonymous.

Outside the walls of the Imperial Palace, the mass of Chinese people was always encouraged to be the same. A sense of self apart from the cultural identity of the masses was difficult to even imagine. One of the first things I learned in China was how to be a part of a collective. Billy and I moved from the midst of one crowd to the next—from crowded train stations onto crowded trains and into crowded streets. I often found my face smothered against someone's chest. But this awkward closeness to strangers never fazed Chinese people. When everything—especially space—was communal, one lost a sense of what was distinctly "yours" and "mine." One unlearns the dimensions and characterizations of one's personal space and personal identity. That is why the Chinese are so ready to make the distinction between the Chinese, as a whole, and anyone who isn't Chinese. One of the first Chinese phrases that Billy could recognize in conversation was wai guo ren. In quickly identifying and labeling him as "other," the Chinese were simultaneously confirming their Chineseness. But when they were confronted with someone who was not quite other and not quite Chinese, it was much more difficult to define their relationship with that person.

On one of our crowded bus rides in China, a man had boarded the bus and caused some excitement. He was about seventy years old. His skin was leathery and brown from the sun, and there were deep-set wrinkles in his face. He was wearing a blue cap—the kind Mao used to wear—and a matching blue quilted jacket. When he smiled, which was often, I saw the rotted teeth sitting in his gums—they were pointing in all different directions, like little tombstones on a faraway hill. I couldn't understand what the fuss was about until I heard him speak.

The words that came out barely sounded Chinese. It could have been a derivative of Mandarin—a dialect—but even then, people would have been able to make out some of the familiar sounds and tones. I looked at the man more closely and noticed that his eyes weren't dark brown like the rest of ours. The color was a glassy gray, and he almost didn't look Asian. He resembled the people whose profiles are on Renminbi bills. Billy suspected that the faces on Chinese bills were depicting the supposed diversity in the Chinese population—the people who looked Central Asian, and some almost Caucasian, were all people (like the Mongols and the Uighurs) over whom the Chinese government presumed power.

The bus monitor was trying to communicate with the old man. She asked him where he wanted to go. He took out a crumpled sheet of paper and handed it to her. It was an address. She pointed to the piece of paper and asked whether this was where he wanted to go. Whenever he answered her questions, he let a river of foreign words rush from his mouth, seemingly oblivious to the fact that no one could understand him. In the mess of his sentences, we all made out one word—Xinjiang. We guessed that this was where the man had come from—this most western province, which cradled Mongolia and bordered Kyrgyzstan, one of the easternmost Central Asian countries.

Immediately, I felt a connection to this man from Xinjiang. The summer I had been in St. Petersburg, a man had come up to me in the street to ask whether I was Tartar. Confused, I had asked Billy why someone might think so. He had explained the connection between Tartars and Mongols and how they had invaded Central Asia and Eastern Europe in the Middle Ages. That is probably why some Chinese people—like this old man from Xinjiang—looked like a mix between Asians and Eastern Europeans. Billy laughed and said that it was more likely because the Russians knew I was Mongolian.

There is a running joke between the two of us that I am really of Mongolian descent. When some Chinese babies are born, it is common for them to have blue birthmarks on their behinds. The saying is that these babies are Mongolian and the blue mark is a bruise caused by the mother kicking her baby out of her womb because she is upset that her baby is not Han Chinese. After about four or five years, though, these birthmarks disappear. I still have two of these marks on the skin over my tailbone. They are sky blue.

I kept watching the man, hoping I could catch his eye and see whether he felt the same strange connection I felt toward him—the feeling of wanting to belong here, all the while knowing that we did not. He looked around the bus, his mouth always half open with a childlike smile and wonder. When his eyes fell upon my face, I opened my eyes wide and smiled at him brightly. He returned the smile, pushing the corners of his mouth into the creases ingrained in his cheeks. And then he continued panning the bus, smiling at whomever his eyes happened to rest on.

Finally, the bus monitor, still holding that piece of paper, reached over and tapped the man on his arm. She said loudly in Chinese, "This here is your stop! You get off here!" She seemed to think that if she spoke louder, he might be able to understand.

The man got up, thanked the bus monitor by grasping her upper arm firmly, and got off the bus. As he descended the steps, he looked back and smiled at the bus and waved good-bye. We watched through the dirty windows as he walked, without any hesitation, in a direction that may or may not have led him to his destination.

I remember now that there was an expectation on my part, to experience some kind of revelation after my trip to China. I was hoping for one that would bring me closer to my Chineseness; I had anticipated all the emotions of a homecoming. "Overseas Chinese," people who were born and raised elsewhere, often write about their experiences of going to China, journeys that almost always conclude with a feeling of wholeness, of being made complete. My good friend Bindy, who had been adopted by an American family as part of Operation Babylift after the Vietnam War, told me she felt a strange and wonderful sense of belonging she had never felt before the first time she went to Vietnam when she was twenty years old. When she described her "homecoming" to me, I could easily empathize—I imagined this must be how I would feel on my first trip to China. I blindly assumed that the root of my identity was Chinese, and not Taiwanese, because China was so much larger than Taiwan, its history so much longer—because Chineseness seemed to precede Taiwaneseness. But I had been wrong. Going to China did not feel like a homecoming; my journey made me feel all the more Taiwanese, all the more American, and only a little bit Chinese.

I have asked myself what I considered the most memorable moment on my first trip to China. It was not when Billy and I stood in one of the guard towers of the Great Wall and could understand how people could wholeheartedly believe that this structure was all it would take to protect the Middle Kingdom from invaders. It was not when we went on a boat ride on Xihu—"West Lake"—in Hangzhou and, as we glided across the glassy surface of the water, our rower recited ancient Chinese poetry for us. It was not when we climbed to the top of the Nanjing city gates and met two old men who were sitting on a small plot of grass, smoking and flying a red kite. The most memorable moment for me on this trip was when I learned how to ride a bicycle in Qufu.

Qufu was Confucius' birthplace. There is a forest named after him where he and all his descendants are buried. To see everything inside the forest and, most importantly, to find Confucius' tomb, you have to rent a bicycle at the front gates of the forest.

I had had a bicycle once. I was five. There's a picture of me riding around the Chiang Kai-shek Memorial in Taipei while wearing pink earmuffs. There were two training wheels attached to the back wheel, and my father had told me that they would, with time, automatically lift off the ground and, without even realizing it, I would know how to ride a bicycle. But there was never another bicycle excursion to the memorial. My parents had been too busy and Taipei's traffic too hectic for there to have been another trip. My bicycle had remained abandoned in the dank storage room in the basement of our apartment, and I never learned how to ride.

When I was about seven or eight, I was also forced to memorize some of Confucius' analects. Because my brother and I were always enrolled in American schools, our parents had hired tutors to teach us Chinese at home;

it was imperative that my brother and I speak Chinese fluently. I detested memorization exercises. But our tutor made us memorize Chinese poetry and a few lines of Confucius' sayings. Whenever it was time for this, I would crawl under the desk and refuse to come out until our hour was up. In the end, my tutor quit her job because she told my mother she didn't deserve to get paid when I hadn't learned a thing.

We had to cross two gates before we entered the Confucius Forest. Between the two gates was a stretch of paved road. We decided that this would be a good place for me to learn how to ride a bicycle before going onto the bumpy forest terrain. I got on my bike and took a few deep breaths. I knew how the motions of riding a bicycle looked; I even thought I could will myself into believing that I already knew how to do this—that maybe there hadn't been any training wheels on my bicycle in Taipei. But as soon as I lifted both feet off the ground, I lost balance and my feet came pounding down on the pavement. Billy cycled by leisurely and said, "It's been so long since I've ridden a bike!" I looked at him and rolled my eyes.

"I feel stupid," I said. People were sitting along the road, all of them taking a break from riding their bicycles in the forest. I heard some snickering. I was probably the first Chinese person they'd seen who didn't know how to ride a bicycle. I could feel my face get hot. Billy rode back toward me.

"What'd you say? I couldn't hear you."

"I said, I feel stupid."

"You don't look stupid," Billy said. "Here, let's try something different." He told me to place both feet on the pedals.

"I can't! Didn't you just see me? I'll fall!" I shrieked.

"You won't," he said, "I'm going to hold on. I won't let you fall." I was terribly conscious of the people watching us now that it was absolutely clear I didn't know how to ride a bicycle. But I put both feet on the pedals and made a few wobbly revolutions. Billy told me to keep doing that. I did, and the more I pedaled, the more I picked up speed. I straightened my back, moved forward with my bicycle, and glided forward a good twenty feet.

"Squeeze the brakes on your handlebars!" Billy's voice came from far behind. I slowed down and let my right foot drop and skip forward three steps before I turned around. Billy was standing twenty feet behind me with his arms across his chest, smiling.

I rode back and forth along the pavement before we cycled past the second gate into the Confucius Forest. I followed Billy's lead and bumped along the dirt road. There were tall signposts that pointed toward Confucius' tomb. All the tourists on their bicycles were going in that direction. Billy and I went in the opposite direction, and soon it was just the two of us cycling into the forest. There were trees and dried grass on either side of the dirt road and an abandoned wheelbarrow off to the right. Almost without warning, the forest opened into a field of vibrant purple flowers. I rode behind Billy, laughing to myself as my legs pedaled happily.

We rode deeper and deeper into the forest. Tombstones were dispersed alongside the road. All of them bore names that began with the character Kong, Confucius' surname. The forest was quiet and still, and all I could hear was the sound of the wind rushing by my ears as I pedaled my bicycle. It was here that I felt the palpable connection to the past—the cultural legacy of ancient China.

That night, I called my father from our hotel and told him that we were in Qufu and that I had learned how to ride a bicycle. He laughed into the phone.

"Really?" His voice was broken up with static, but I could recognize his genuine excitement for me. "That's wonderful, xiao bao! And how appropriate that you are in Qufu—it is as if Confucius himself taught you."

HOME

It was Billy's idea to spend the summer in Taiwan. We were in his apartment in Washington, D.C., where he was in his first year of law school. I was folding clothes or straightening the sheets—something—when he said, "Let's go to Taiwan this summer." I stiffened and then continued what I was doing and did not give him a sign that I'd heard him. Sometimes, when we are lying in bed, talking, I will close my eyes in the middle of a difficult conversation and pretend I have fallen asleep. What Billy calls my "ostrich instinct" is something I have inherited from my mother, though thankfully, I am not as stubborn as she is in avoiding an issue, because eventually, I always open my eyes and resume our conversation. My mother will look blankly at me—almost through me—as if I have not uttered a single word to her.

"Hello? Did you hear me?" Billy reached out for me. "You don't think it's a good idea." His voice fell.

I looked up, into his face. "No," I began, "it's a good idea. But it's complicated too."

There would be too many expectations from my parents. Parents' normal hopes for their children to eventually return home and settle down is more acute for my parents because the implications of my not coming back to Taiwan are that I will ultimately be of a different nationality and a different culture from them. My brother, after spending four years at Cornell and one and a half years between Chicago and London, moved to Hong Kong in 1997, the year of the Handover, and there are no signs of his leaving Asia. He visits my parents every two weeks; they are not worried about him. For the six years I have been away from home, I have been back about once every year and stay for only two to three weeks at a time—just enough time to leave home feeling that there hadn't been enough time—partly wistful about the brevity of my trip and partly grateful that there hadn't been a chance for my parents' questions about when I would be coming to live in Taiwan.

I have friends who are afraid to go home for more than two weeks, lest their parents forbid them to leave again. For some, going home is a trap because the familiarity and comfort of home can become burdensome. There are too few unknowns, too many conveniences. Or we have changed too much to be able to reconcile the people we have become after leaving Taiwan with the people our parents shaped us to become before leaving Taiwan. A friend of mine once complained, "Every time I go home to Taiwan, I get all confused—everything that I am so sure about when I am on my own gets thrown on its head and turned upside down. I no longer know whether what's important to me is important because I think it is or if it's important because my parents think it is." For me, perhaps not wanting to go home yet is just a function of my age. I am too young to return somewhere; it is too soon to retrace my steps.

The other reason for my ambivalence about spending the summer in Taiwan was Billy. There would be a lot of pressure on him, and on us. Even if my parents had somewhat grasped and partially accepted the idea of our relationship, there was the rest of their social circle to whom Billy and I and my parents would have to answer. Taipei is a small city where my parents have lived for more than fifty years—a period of time over which they have made many friends. Though their circle of friends is large, it is still small enough—as any social circle is—to be easily excited by gossip. My parents usually stand outside from that kind of petty talk, in large part because they have a solid, even paradigmatic, marriage and two children who have not done anything worth whispering about. But spending three months at home with my boyfriend would be just the kind of thing to set off alarm bells.

"I know it won't be easy," Billy said, "but it will be wonderful."

I looked at him. He was smiling, thinking about all the possibilities of spending the summer in Taiwan—how the trip would open up the way he understands me. Before meeting him in Russia, I had always felt as though I had to footnote everything I told people about my background. Because I felt that most people would rather ignore the tedium of reading the scrawny black print of footnotes and instead head straight to the larger words in the main body of a text, I had stopped trying to explain. This made it both easier and more difficult to relate to people. My life growing up in Taiwan became a secret, almost nonexistent, life because I rarely talked about it in detail. A very clear and definite split erupted between my life at home in Taiwan and my life at school in America. But with Billy, there was never this feeling of having to explain myself. Somehow, he got it right away. He understood the nuances of my particular history, my particular culture, and even the particularities of my family. It was such a relief to have someone understand, to be able to reconcile the split between Taiwan and America.

Before Billy and I had gone to China, we had spent four short days in Taiwan with my parents. They had both been cordial but not warm with him. My mother, especially, was guarded, and when she smiled at him, it was a meek half-smile that quivered in the corners with resistance. When Billy and I had had time alone, I had apologized for her coldness, and he had told me, "Don't be sorry. These things take time—we have to get to know each other first." And for the rest of our stay in Taiwan, Billy had been careful about giving my mother the time and space to make the decision about wanting to get to know him.

I began thinking, too, about the possibilities of going home with Billy for the summer. There were so many things from home that I had only told him about—things that remained a part of my secret, guarded life in Taiwan because no one from my life here in America had ever witnessed them. He had already shared his past with me by showing me where he had grown up in San Diego and even the house his family had lived in for three years in New Mexico. Home for Billy seemed so concrete to me—there was that empty lot that his father had told him was the site where ancient pirate treasures were buried. There was his elementary school—a low, grey, Lego-like structure that sat atop a small hill overlooking palm trees. There was Double Happiness, the Chinese restaurant where his family went and ordered volcano shrimp—a dish I had never tried, so I was sure it was some made-up American concoction like chop suey until Billy and I went to Shanghai and ordered it at a restaurant. And there was the stretch of satiny beach just down the hill from the house where he had grown up. Our trips to San Diego and New Mexico had deepened my understanding of him because it showed me Billy in the context of his home, and our trips also deepened his understanding of me because it placed me in the context of his home.

I softened, "It would be wonderful, wouldn't it?"

Billy's eyes lit up. "Yes! You could finally work on your mother's book, and I can intern at a law firm, and we could travel around the island, and— it's just going to be great. I know it."

The year before, my mother had told me she was writing a book of essays on her collection of antique woven baby carriers from Chinese tribes and she wanted me to translate her work into English. During my first year of graduate school, I had time only to translate one of her essays. If I spent the summer at home, she and I would be able to complete this project. And then to travel around Taiwan with Billy! Suddenly, the prospect of being at home for the summer excited me. Billy was right—we couldn't deny that there would inevitably be awkward moments when we were in Taiwan, but we also couldn't deny ourselves the opportunity to be there together. So we decided we would spend the summer of 2000 in Taiwan.

I called my parents over Christmas to tell them our plan. I was spending the holidays with Billy's family in San Diego.

"Oh," my mother said. "Well." She tried not to sound surprised, but she did sound hurt.

"Anyway, Mom, I just wanted to tell you 'Merry Christmas' and all that," I said quickly. "I'll call again soon."

My mother called me in late January when I was back in school in New York.

"You know," she began, "that 'that person' can't stay with us this summer, right? Not even in the Taipei apartment." After I'd left for college, my parents had moved out of our apartment in Taipei to a fishing port called Tamsui. "That person" was Billy.

"Oh," I said. "Well." I felt my eyes get hot and my throat tighten.

"I just think it would be asking too much of us if he stayed in our house. It would make me feel very uncomfortable."

"Well, thanks for letting me know," I replied coldly. As soon as I hung up the phone, I began to cry, feeling that my mother had rejected me and Billy without having ever given us a chance. I called Billy right away. He was silent after I told him what my mother had said.

"What are you thinking?"

"That maybe it's not such a good idea anymore," he said. His tone was flat, dejected; it frightened me.

"That's not true!" I cried. "She just needs some time. She's just not used to all this and doesn't know how to react. You said yourself that we have to be patient because it's going to take time for you and my parents to get to know each other."

"I know." He was quiet. I went on to tell him all the reasons he should give my mother a chance. Suddenly, it was on her behalf that I was asking for Billy's understanding.

"Listen," he finally said, "I was just now seeing how difficult an entire summer in Taiwan might be. I mean, right now, this phone call with your mother—it's already the first hurdle we have to go over, and it's only January! We haven't even set foot in Taiwan yet. Do you still think we should go home this summer?"

"Yes," I said firmly. "Yes, I do. I am sure of it now."

"Even knowing that we will have to deal with a lot of this, this stuff?"

"Yes. We have to deal with my mother sooner or later. That'll all work itself out in time—you said that, remember? Anyway, that's secondary to all the good things that will come out of going home this summer." I was talking loudly. "Right?"

"You're right." Billy relaxed.

The truth was, we couldn't close our eyes in mid-conversation and hope that a difficult issue would just disappear.

In the following months, Billy wrote to several law firms in Taipei, and finally, my father—who was, after his heart surgery, much more open to my relationship with Billy than my mother—helped him land a job as an intern in one of the largest Taiwanese law firms. My mother and I had a few more awkward exchanges about the living arrangements, and I assured her that once we arrived at home, Billy and I would start looking for an apartment for him. My father, excited to hear that I was coming home, called and said, "There are a lot of things I need you to do for the company. You'll come work for me."

"I will?" I laughed. "Doing what? I don't know anything about business!"

"Don't be so sure. We'll discuss it when you come home."

In late May, Billy and I flew from New York to Tokyo and then from Tokyo to Taipei. On the plane, Billy watched all four movies and read the paper to review the latest news on the recent presidential elections in Taiwan two months before; I had told him that my father was sure to test his knowledge on the subject. When the plane was only an hour away from Taipei and our eighteen-hour trip was coming to an end, Billy looked over at me, his eyes red and dry. "I don't think I could talk about politics right now." He had not slept the entire flight and was just now feeling drowsy.

"But you can't just go right to sleep when we arrive. My parents will have a whole meal of congee and vegetables and soup and fruits laid out waiting for us."

"Wha—? I can't eat right now." He could barely keep his eyes open. Immediately, I felt myself begin to panic. I was afraid that if he didn't stay up for dinner, my parents would judge him and think him disrespectful and impolite.

"Just eat a little bit," I said, trying to sound calm. "It's a ritual—warm food for travelers coming home."

Billy nodded lazily and let his heavy eyelids drop.

When we got home, my father opened the large, wooden door to our apartment in Tamsui. It was already eleven o'clock at night, but he and my mother hadn't eaten dinner yet. They were waiting for us to have congee together.

"I'm starving!" My father said as he hugged me tightly. We pulled apart, and he reached out behind me to shake Billy's hand. "Hello," he said, holding Billy's hand firmly. "It's good to see you again." My father smiled up at Billy, who stood six inches taller than my father and a foot taller than my mother and me. My mother—looking somewhat reluctant—walked slowly toward me in her slippers and held me limply. She patted my back a few times.

"Did you have a long trip?" She asked Billy, holding her hand out to him.

"Yes, it was long." Billy took her hand. "We're glad to finally be here, though." He had looked in my direction when he used the "we" pronoun, and I nervously wondered whether my mother would find that presumptuous of him. I wondered if she thought that he was overstepping boundaries because she, my father, and I deserved the "we" treatment more than he and I did.

When my father announced again that he was hungry and that we should quickly wash our hands so that we could eat, I was relieved—not because I was in the least bit hungry, but because it made me uncomfortable to see the small exchange between Billy and my mother. They were both cautiously studying each other. Billy looked for signs that told him how friendly he could be with my mother, while my mother looked him up and down and silently made judgments. When Billy reached over to carry my bags down the hall, I checked to see if my mother had caught that. She had, and was nodding, ever so slightly, to herself.

After we put our bags in our rooms—Billy was to stay in my brother's room next to mine—we came back out into the dining room with the round, dark wood table upon which steaming plates of food were placed around the lazy susan. All the foods I'd told Billy about were there. Our conversation throughout dinner was in English, though a few times, I broke into Chinese, not wanting my parents to think that Billy would be made uncomfortable if we spoke in Chinese with each other. His Mandarin was good enough for him to pick out certain words and know, roughly, what we were talking about. He knew when to smile and laugh, when to nod, and when to answer back, though he had to reply in English. He had also taken a semester of Taiwanese at Berkeley and had learned a random string of vocabulary words—names of fruits and vegetables and body parts, and phrases like, "I am American," "Are you a teacher?" And my favorite—the equivalent to "How are you?"—"Have you eaten?"

It was less than twenty minutes into our conversation when my father brought up the election. It was the first time since Chiang Kai-shek's Nationalist government came to Taiwan in 1949 that the opposition party had won an election. The Democratic Progressive Party (DPP) was known for its strong stand for Taiwan's independence. Ever since the new president, Chen Shui-bian, had been elected into office, China had been scrutinizing Taiwan's every move even more closely, threatening to use force if the island made a move toward independence. In 1996, after Taiwan's first full-blown democratic election, China had lobbed missiles dangerously and precariously close to the island.

"I heard that after A-mei sang the national anthem at the inauguration,"

Billy offered, "China pulled down billboards of her on the mainland and refused to sell or play her music anymore." A-mei was a Taiwanese pop singer who was also popular in China.

My father looked at me, opened his eyes wide and smiled, nodding his head in approval. "Eh! He's not bad!"

We asked questions about the inauguration, and my mother told me that she had clipped President Chen's speech from a newspaper and left it in my room. She described the ceremony—how it had begun with Taiwanese aboriginal dancers jumping together in circles and beating on drums, followed by an elegantly delivered farewell speech by President Lee Teng-hui, and finally, Chen's speech describing his victory as first and foremost a victory for democracy. My mother's nose got red as she spoke, and when she finished, she blinked her eyes quickly.

When Chen had won the election in March, Billy and I were in my apartment in New York, which I shared with two friends from Taiwan. My roommates and I took turns with the telephone, calling our parents in Taiwan, each of us handing the phone to the next red-nosed and teary-eyed person. That the opposition party had won proved that Taiwan was now truly a full democracy. That night, Taiwanese citizens heaved a collective, satisfactory sigh as they looked into the past and saw how far they had come.

Over mangoes and apple pears, we talked about our plans for the next few days before work started for Billy and me. I told my parents that we would set out to look for an apartment to sublet for Billy.

"It's not going to be easy," my father said. "Subletting isn't such a common thing in Taipei. If you still don't have a place by the time your job starts, Billy—" My mother shot a look at my father, but he didn't acknowledge her and continued. "You can stay in our Taipei apartment." Billy and I glanced at each other quickly.

"That's very nice of you, Mr. Lin," Billy nodded his head at my father. "Thank you." And then he said in my mother's direction, "I'll try to find a place as soon as possible."

There was silence for a few minutes, and then I scooted back from the table and told my parents that it was late and that we should probably all go to bed. They nodded, Billy got up with me, and we went toward our rooms.

Almost as soon as Billy fell on top of my brother's futon mattress on the floor, he was asleep.

"Come wake me up in the morning," he mumbled.

"Good night." I smiled at his half-closed eyes and stood up to leave.

"I'm happy to be here. I can't believe we made it," Billy called sleepily after me.

"I know; I'm happy, too."

In my room, I unpacked my bags and put my clothes into the closet. Because my parents had moved to Tamsui after my first year of college, I had never stayed in this apartment long enough to unpack my suitcase. The clothes that were already hanging in the closet were a few dresses that I had worn to high school dances. They were covered in thin, silky plastic from the dry cleaner's. My mother had used the rest of the empty closet space for storage—long, skinny rolls of wrapping paper, boxes of soaps and perfumes she kept handy to give away as presents, and an old mint-green and pale-pink aerobics step that my aunt had brought to Taiwan when step aerobics had been popular in the States. In the back of the closet, some of my grandfather's paintings were stacked up against my old drawings. At some point, my mother had taken all my best paintings from high school and college, framed them, and hung them all over the walls in my room and Alex's room in this apartment.

When I was in high school, my mother used to make small changes—like putting up new curtains in the living room and new showerheads in our bathrooms—in our Taipei apartment and not mention them until I noticed. She would smile modestly and ask, "You like it?" And I saw how my mother was so attentive to details and so quiet about the way she made changes to better our lives in small, seemingly insignificant ways. Now I looked around the room—unfamiliar, not lived in, and yet familiar, too, because of all the books, old journals, photo albums, and old letters in it that were mine, which my mother had arranged on the shelves. On the bottom bookshelf was a pile of mail and old *National Geographic* magazines that had been forwarded home after I had graduated college. On top of this pile was a neatly-cut-out newspaper clipping of President Chen's inaugural speech. Over the futon mattress on my floor, my mother had spread a Chinese red silk comforter, which she had made using fabric she had bought on one of her trips to China. I took a deep breath and could smell the faint hint of my mother's perfume. When I was growing up and had friends over, she would make our beds on the floor and spray our pillows with her perfume, transforming my ordinary room into a beautiful, dreamy place. I looked around once more and felt so glad to be spending the summer in this room. In three months, I would make it mine.

The next day while my parents were at work in the office, Billy and I took a walk along the Tamsui River, watching the preparations for the annual dragon boat races. Tamsui is the only town whose English transliteration of its name is derived from Taiwanese, not Mandarin. It is known for its seafood and "old Taiwan" feel; when my grandparents were growing up, Tamsui—not Taipei—was downtown. It is a half-hour north of Taipei, and from the window in my parents' bedroom, you can see across the Taiwan straits, where Mainland China lies. Tamsui was the port through which both sides of my family came to Taiwan from Fukien province in China—four generations ago on my father's side and nineteen generations ago on my mother's side. When I was growing up, the Tamsui River had been notorious for its pungent odor, as there would always be trash drifting in the river. Driving alongside it on the freeway, my brother and I could detect the sulfurous smell of stagnant, dead water, even through closed windows. But over the years, the government cleaned up the river and built up the town of Tamsui; because Tamsui was the northernmost stop on the metro, people from Taipei like to come up over the weekends.

As we walked along the river, Billy and I passed by various vendors, most selling food that we wouldn't be able to get in the city. I bought Billy a bottle of cream soda known as "marble soda"—the kind my father used to drink as a young boy. The bottle was made of thick green glass topped off with a plastic cap. In the middle of the cap was a hole, stopped by a glass marble. Before handing us the bottle, the vendor struck the cap with his palm in one quick, assured movement, and the marble fell with a clink to the bottom of the bottle as tiny bubbles rushed up to the top. He stuck a straw in it—which immediately floated up, slanting out of the bottle—and handed it over to us. He reminded us to return the empty bottle to him or any other "marble soda" vendor when we were finished.

Another vendor was making "dragon whisker candies." In a large, rectangular pan filled with a small mountain of powdered white sugar, he mixed some of the sugar with a thick, syrupy liquid and formed an iridescent, pebble-like ball of hardened syrup. He then began pulling this pebble apart, forming long, thin strands of sugar between his hands. He repeated this a few times, bringing his hands together and out again, multiplying the hair-like strands of sugar, making them thinner and thinner each time he pulled out again. If a crowd drew near, he would take one sugar thread and poke it through the eye of a needle to show us how delicate the sugary hair was. Then he rolled the sugar in sweetened black sesame or sweetened peanut powder and cut the long ribbon of sugar into small square pieces. We bought a box of mixed flavors and chewed the candies slowly, getting the sticky sugar stuck in our teeth.

Out on the river, there was a boatful of rowers practicing for the dragon boat race in a few days. At the head of the thin boat, a man faced the rowers and beat a drum. Every time his wooden stick came pounding down on the taut belly of the drum, we saw the rowers slice their paddles uniformly into the glassy surface of the water. I explained to Billy that the dragon boat races were held every year in honor of the Chinese poet, Qu Yuan, who committed suicide by jumping into a river many, many years ago. After Qu Yuan's suicide, men from the village went out in boats to look for his body, and the women wrapped small portions of rice with lotus leaves for the men to throw into the water. The goal was for the fish, shrimp, and other sea creatures to eat these zong zi instead of Qu Yuan's body. Every year at this time, women wrap zong zi filled with sticky rice, meats, egg yolks, and walnuts and bring them out to the boat races in remembrance of the poet Qu Yuan.

We walked by Sushi-ya, a Japanese restaurant that my parents go to at least once every week. It is my family's favorite place to eat—a Sunday-afternoon or Sunday-night routine. The last time Billy and I were in Taiwan, my parents took us there, and after lunch, Billy exclaimed to me that it was by far the best meal he had ever had. He was sincere; it is unlike Billy to say something he does not mean, even if it might be a white lie, a nice comment that someone might appreciate. I made sure my father heard Billy's exclamation. It wasn't because we needed Billy's confirmation that this hole-in-the-wall sushi place in Tamsui was really top-notch; I just wanted to share with my father that overwhelming sense of accomplishment and satisfaction when something you've always believed to be true is confirmed by someone else with as much conviction and enthusiasm as your own. You marvel and imagine that your belief—your opinion—must be truth itself. Though no one said so, I felt that taking Billy to Sushi-ya was part test, part initiation. Because Billy loved the place as much as my family, it proved that he had passed the test. The first time we went to Sushi-ya, my family and Billy sat at the counter but didn't order. Instead, the idamaii-san, the sushi chef, served us what he deemed the freshest fish and shellfish that day. My father was impressed by Billy's enthusiastic appetite and appreciation for good Taiwanese-Japanese food. After our meal, my father put his hand on Billy's back and slapped it a few times with approval. Later, Billy excitedly asked if I had seen that gesture. When we returned to the States, Billy couldn't stop reminiscing about the meal we had at Sushi-ya, and now we could go whenever we wanted to.

Billy and I walked into the small restaurant and sat at a table. The idamaii-san didn't recognize us, and neither did the waitress. We ordered some fish and a few rolls, and shared a bottle of Kirin. We drank to "summer in Taiwan" and ate off the thick wooden blocks.

"See," Billy said, after putting a piece of hamachi in his mouth, so fresh that it almost melted on his tongue. "This right here is one of the good things that makes all the difficult and awkward moments all right."

A few days later, after we had already had some trouble finding a place for Billy (the first "apartment" we had looked at was a basement storage room for spare tires underneath a car shop), we decided to move him to the Taipei apartment because work would start soon, and Tamsui was too far for him to commute to work in downtown Taipei. The morning after Billy moved to Taipei, my mother called me into her room.

"Bon Bon's mother wants to invite us to dinner tonight," she told me. Bon Bon was my good friend, Yvonne. Our families had been close friends for three generations—our grandmothers were so close that when my aunt, Meiguo Ah-ma's oldest daughter, was still a baby, Yvonne's grandmother had breast-fed her when Meiguo Ah-ma was too busy working in the hospital. When I go through old pictures of my parents, I often see Helena, Yvonne's mother, in them. Yvonne looked just like her mother when she was young with the same thick, arched eyebrows, sharp chin, and perfectly flirtatious smile.

"Okay," I said. My mother was looking at me, troubled.

"She wants to invite 'that person' too."

"You mean Billy."

"You know, Judy will be there, too. And Sue." Judy was a friend of my parents, and Sue was my godmother. My mother's tone was expectant, waiting for me to have some kind of a reaction.

"That's nice," I said.

"Do you know what Judy asked me earlier on the phone?" She furrowed her eyebrows, looking hurt and offended. I shook my head. "She asked if she would be meeting my future son-in-law tonight." My mother said "future son-in-law" as though it were a dirty word.

"What?" I couldn't believe my mother's friend was already talking and provoking her like this.

"Exactly!" She said, exasperated. "And what was I supposed to say to that? I didn't know what to say!"

"You don't have to say anything, Mom."

"What does that mean? Is there something going on that I don't know about? You know how I hate finding out things about my children through other people. It's embarrassing not knowing what's going on with my own children." She shook her head back and forth, her face stricken with a look of genuine grief and fear. I began thinking about the reasons why I wouldn't be able to live in Taiwan in the future—this was one of them. My mother often reminded me how "inconvenient" it would be to marry someone who was not also Taiwanese. Once, she even went so far as to give me a few names of her friends with whom she would not mind becoming in-laws. A few months before Billy and I had arrived in Taiwan, my mother had called and asked me whether all of Billy's previous girlfriends had been Asian, and I bristled, thinking about what she was insinuating.

"Mom." I tried to be as calm as possible, even though I could already feel my face get hot. It was difficult to be as articulate, and even reasonable, having this conversation in Chinese. But if I let myself go into English, I was afraid that the real conversation we were having—that being with Billy made me too "American" and that ultimately, being with him meant I might never live in Taiwan again—would be made more pronounced and too obvious to bear. "I'm sorry about what Auntie Judy said. She would never know something before I tell you myself, Mom. Believe me."

"Is that true? I don't know. All I know is that all of this—all of this is putting a lot of pressure on me. It's making me very uncomfortable! I just don't know what you want from me."

I flinched. "All of this" referred to Billy and me—our relationship and this beautiful thing that we shared and that I wanted to show my parents—and all my mother could feel was how discomforting it was. I was reacting and thinking in English and simultaneously had to translate my thoughts into Chinese, and in the midst of all that, I suddenly broke down. It hurt so much to sit across from my mother and hear her say how unhappy my relationship with Billy made her. She was making me feel guilty about being with Billy, as though I were doing something terribly wrong by being with him. But as much as this angered and saddened me, I did not have the courage to call up these words to say to her.

"I'm sorry," I said lamely.

"Why are you crying? I don't understand."

"I'm sorry that I'm doing something to make you feel this way," I managed to get out. "If you could just tell me what it is I am doing wrong. . . . "

She fell silent. I couldn't read the expression on her face—I couldn't tell if she was glaring at me or reconsidering. Then my father rushed into the room. We must have raised our voices so that he had heard us from the living room. He stood by the bed and looked at my mother. "Why don't you just say what you are really thinking? Just come out and say it!"

She looked up at him, a look of betrayal on her face. "What are you talking about?"

"Why don't you just admit that you can't bear the thought of our daughter being with someone who isn't Taiwanese!"

The three of us froze. We were all shocked by the nakedness of the truth my father had uttered. It was something we all knew, and the real issue that my mother and I were talking around, without saying it in so many words—not wanting to embarrass each other that way. But my father's words lingered in the air, and I stared at him, and suddenly I heard what he'd said again, ringing in my ears, and I started to cry. I felt like a character in an Amy Tan novel, suffering the horrible cliché of having an unrelentingly traditional and narrow-minded mother. In a way, I felt worse thinking of that analogy because I was far from being that cliché—my mother was not narrow-minded and relentless the way Chinese mothers are often portrayed. If she were, that might have made it easier; the boundaries would have been drawn clearly. But my parents had raised me to be mindful of the world at large, in effect, to think beyond race—beyond culture, even. Her resistance to my being with Billy confused me and pained me all the more because it called into question everything she had taught me. No one said anything for a long time. The three of us were motionless, like little plastic figures in a diorama. We knew that whoever made the first move would be the first to say something. Neither my mother nor I were prepared for my father tearing away the cloak of silence and baring the truth. My mother felt betrayed by my father; I felt the palpable shame of my own mother's prejudice, and the heavy burden of guilt, for making my mother feel "uncomfortable."

My father was the first to move, and then he sat down next to me and took my hand. "Xiao bao, you don't think that Daddy and Mommy don't have any expectations for your future, do you?"

I shook my head.

"We can't help wishing we could keep you here close by, especially when it feels more and more like you might eventually live far away from us." He handed me a tissue. "Remember what I am about to tell you." I looked into my father's face, his eyebrows drooping, his eyes dark and glistening. "Your mother and I are bound to have certain things we want for you—we can't help that. But know that our selfish hopes will always be secondary to what you want for yourself. We will always respect that." He squeezed my hand, and I left for my room, afraid to turn around to face my mother.

Dinner with Auntie Helena, Auntie Judy, Auntie Sue, Yvonne, and Yvonne's grandparents turned out fine in the end. Billy and I had a long talk in the afternoon and agreed that we had to be patient and act as normally as possible when around my mother. He reminded me that the circumstances would be difficult for my mother even if I had brought home someone who was Taiwanese—the fact that I was bringing home a serious boyfriend was something any parent would have a hard time grappling with. So Billy drank and smiled every time Yvonne's grandfather, who seemed completely in his own world and who, because he sat directly across from Billy at the round table, continually raised his glass to him across the table. We all laughed when my father told jokes. Yvonne and I made plans to call our friend Jackie and go out after dinner.

After dinner, we said good-bye to all the aunties and my parents, and Yvonne brought us to a new bar called Mao's Café. The bar was small and dark when we first walked in; we had to go up a flight of narrow stairs to get to the bigger bar area upstairs. All along the walls up the stairs were framed Mao Zedong paraphernalia: T-shirts, little red books, Mao lighters, records of Mao's teachings. A lot of these things, Billy and I had seen (and he had bought) when we had visited Shaoshan, Mao's birthplace. But seeing Mao's image in the context of Taiwan made apparent to us the country's willingness and readiness to let the past go. Billy stopped in front of one particular glass case and laughed. In the case, against a red felt background, were many little Mao pins arranged into the shape of Taiwan.

"The Taiwanese have a great sense of humor," Billy remarked.

"Oh, wait till you go to the bathroom!" Yvonne smiled knowingly.

In front of the entranceway to the men's and women's bathrooms was a big red rectangle covered in fuzzy, shag carpet material—it was about four feet high and three feet wide and spun around on a pole. On one side of the rectangle was a large picture of Mao, and on the other side was Chiang Kai-shek. Both photographs, because they were so big, made the men look silly and comical. They took turns smiling toothily at us as we spun the rectangle around.

Of all my childhood friends, I had always thought Yvonne would be the most well adjusted to resuming life at home. Her parents hadn't put her in American school until she was in the eighth grade. She spoke the most fluent Mandarin and Taiwanese and was well-read in Chinese literature. Even now, after graduating college, when most of us had long ago abandoned the study of Chinese after we'd reached a satisfying junior high level of reading and writing, she continued to read novels and comic books in Chinese. It was a task I could never accomplish, as I easily became impatient when I tried because I read so slowly in Chinese and would quickly exchange the Chinese book in my hand for an English one.

Yvonne had had a childhood quite different from mine. Her life in a Taiwanese school classroom had inspired different stories of growing up, and I often asked her to share these with me. With a strange longing, I listened to her tell stories of surreptitiously stealing tea eggs from her classmates' tin lunch boxes—it was the same longing with which I listened to my father tell stories of his youth. In fact, Yvonne and my father had attended the same elementary school, and it was not without a tinge of jealousy that I regarded them when she and my father swapped stories about school—pranks, cheating strategies, even teachers whom they had shared. But now, as Yvonne slouched on the bar stool, wearing a sweater set, khakis, and wedge sandals, stirring her Chivas and Coke with a little red straw, she candidly spoke about the pressures of living at home.

"Why don't you come back to the States, then?"

"I can't!" She cried. "Not yet, anyway. You're lucky because you've got cool parents. Even though, deep down, we all know that your parents ultimately want you to come home to settle down, they would never say it to your face. They would never give you that kind of pressure."

Yvonne was right. One thing my father had always felt uncomfortable doing was putting pressure on another person—especially family. Even though I knew that, in his heart, he would be deeply moved if Alex or I took the initiative to declare ourselves Taiwanese citizens and move home forever, he has never asked us to do so. My mother, on the other hand, has asked me hypothetical questions like, "Whose side would you be on if the United States went to war with Taiwan?" Choose one, she was begging, the right one. Even though my mother tried to tell us, as indirectly as she could, what she wanted for our future, it was to our father's delicate silence that we listened, willingly and respectfully.

I thought about what had happened earlier that morning. When my father had taken my hand and admitted to me that he and my mother would always have selfish desires for me, he hadn't spelled out what these wishes were, only that he couldn't help having them. What he didn't say was this: Of course, like my mother, my father would prefer that I eventually live at home and be with someone who is also Taiwanese—someone with whom my family could laugh and joke with in all the languages that we speak, someone who would understand, without explanation, all the cultural nuances that make our family unique. But he couldn't, and would never, ask that of me because he loves me too much to define my happiness. For my part, I have learned from my father and knew that I shouldn't have to ask my parents to give Billy and me a chance. Billy's understanding and appreciation of me—and of our family—was something I knew that my parents would come to see with time.

"Hey." Yvonne suddenly slid off from her bar stool. "There's Jackie!"

I turned to see our friend walk into the bar. The last time I had seen Jackie was over more than a year before when I had visited her in Portland, Oregon, where she had worked in advertising after graduating from Lewis and Clark College. Shortly after my visit, she had moved to Taipei and has since been working in a Taiwanese advertising firm and living at home. She looked the same—happy and laughing, her nose crinkled at the bridge as her eyes squinted into little slits, her mouth opened in a generous hello. She said my name, but quickly turned to Billy and, this being the first time the two of them had met, threw her thin arms around him and said, "Gosh, I feel like I know you already!" Then the two of us hugged for a very long time. It felt good to be with my childhood friends in the context of home. Even though during college, we had been spread all over the States attending different schools, we still considered each other our closest friends, and during Thanksgiving breaks, as our college friends flew home for the long weekend, we always picked one city and flew there to spend the holidays with one another. When we were away from home, we were one another's surrogate family.

Jackie ordered a beer and pulled over a stool from another table.

"How are you? How are you?"

"How are *you?*" I asked. Jackie knew I was referring to her move home.

"I'm well!" Jackie said brightly. "I'm doing surprisingly well." She and Yvonne exchanged a knowing look. "Of course, it's not always easy living at home. But considering, I am really enjoying my life here—I actually have a life here! Who knew that could happen?"

Of our friends, the contrast between Jackie's background and Yvonne's background was probably the starkest. While Yvonne had grown up in Taiwan and gone to Taiwanese school, Jackie had grown up in New Jersey. Jackie had teased her bangs until they stood two inches above her head, used aerosol hairspray, and went to gymnastics practice after school. Her favorite bands in middle school had been Bon Jovi and Whitesnake. Her family hadn't moved back to Taiwan (Jackie was born on the island but left for the United States soon afterward) until we were sophomores in high school. Though Jackie had adapted quickly to life in Taiwan, taking elementary Chinese classes and adding Taiwanese pop singers to her collection of favorite bands, none of us would have guessed that she would want to come back to Taiwan to live. She still seemed much more in tune with her American identity than she was with her Taiwanese side. Or perhaps it was that we had too quickly assumed that because the bulk of her life had been spent in the States, she would identify better with that part of her life, that part of her culture.

"It was difficult in the beginning," Jackie was saying. "I had to lug this huge English-Chinese, Chinese-English dictionary around with me wherever I went. I stayed at work late every night just so I could understand the reports I was given to read. Soon—and I know this makes it sound much easier than it was—I found I could read Chinese very quickly, and then before I knew it, I was giving presentations in Chinese!"

Looking at my friend sitting next to me, taking a swig of her Corona, I saw a slightly different Jackie. "What about your social life? There's just you and Yvonne now back at home. Do you have friends from work?"

"Of course! And so does Yvonne." Jackie laughed. "Don't let her fool you when she tells you how miserable she is here. Yvonne has plenty of friends. In fact, she probably connects better with her coworkers than I do with mine. I mean, Yvonne is practically one of them—she can easily find similar reference points when she talks to people who have grown up here and went to Taiwanese school." I looked at Yvonne. Her lips curled up a little in defense.

"I guess that's true," she began slowly. "But to me, all that is surface fun, surface understanding, and surface connection. Deep down, I still feel I am so different from people here because of my education in the States."

"Maybe," Billy considered, "you feel especially different because you were once so similar to these people. Maybe Jackie has less pressure to connect to people here on a very intimate level because she is different."

"I think Billy's right," Jackie said. "I think people are more willing to accept my differences because they see me as a foreigner. With Yvonne, there's so many more expectations because they see you as one of them."

I looked at the three of us—Jackie sitting on one side of me, and Yvonne on the other. We represented some kind of cultural identity continuum that started with Jackie on the American side and moved closer and closer to Yvonne, who sat at the end of the Taiwanese side. I was somewhere in between: I didn't have Yvonne's pressures to be completely Taiwanese, nor did I have Jackie's freedom to choose how much or how little to assimilate and adapt, but I did have my own uncertainties about being in Taiwan. Maybe I felt toward home the same ambivalence most people felt—that simultaneous push from and pull toward the place and culture they come from. But however comfortable or uncomfortable we each felt at home in Taiwan—however Taiwanese or American we felt we were, or should be, Taiwan would always be the place where we come from—the home that will precede all future homes, even if it was a place we might choose never to return to again.

"Anyway," Yvonne said, "I'm applying to business school, so I'll be back in the States soon enough. When I start my apps, will you help me with my personal statements?"

Billy and I nodded, and she told us she would keep an eye out for apartments for Billy. Soon afterward, we said good night to Yvonne and Jackie; they both had to go to work early the next morning. A week went by, and as it turned out, Yvonne had trouble finding apartment sublets for Billy, too. The next time Billy and I went to Sushi-ya for Sunday night dinner with my parents, he explained the apartment situation to them and apologized for having to stay at our Taipei apartment. After Billy left Tamsui that night, my father came to my room to say good-night and told me, "You probably won't find a place for Billy to rent for just two months."

"I know. What should we do?"

"Don't worry about it—just keep 'looking' for Mommy's sake." I remained quiet, feeling too thankful for my father's understanding to be able to say thank you. He stood by the door, leaning against his elbow. I could see his tanned scalp through his thinning hair. "Okay?" He put his hand on my light switch. I nodded. "Good night," he said and turned off my light.

In June, I began working for my father, and Billy started working at Lee and Li, the Taiwanese law firm where a good friend of my father was a partner. My father wanted me to help him research parenting Web sites and draw up a proposal for a site in Chinese that his children's clothing company would host. I was also in charge of translating documents, letters, and catalogs. It didn't matter to my father that I knew nothing about the Internet industry. But I knew it mattered to him that I made an effort to understand the work he did and the company he had built up on his own thirty years ago. In a way, I was also "putting in my time," even though I had always known that the responsibility of taking the company from my father would not be mine. Or, at least, that was what we all believed—this honor (and burden?) was something my family assumed was reserved for Alex, the son.

But it made my father happy to see me in his office, I knew. Even if I was just typing up correspondence for him or looking through his daily e-mails or browsing on the Internet, looking at parenting Web sites, my mere presence somehow pulled us closer. Sometimes I caught him smiling at me as he peered over his reading glasses to see what I was doing. And when I saw him, he would pretend to look stern and tell me to go back to work. It was important to him that I saw what it had taken for him to get where he is today—to see him in the context of his life's work. We both knew that I would never have the business mind to be very directly involved with his company. Occasionally, I fantasized, as I'm sure my parents did, of being the "perfect" daughter—of coming home after a few more years in the States and working at my father's company, marrying some Taiwanese man who was highly positioned in the company, who played golf with my father and appreciated all the jokes he told over dinner and who inspired my mother to gush and coo over him and brag about him to all her friends. But my parents had raised me to lead a different kind of life—one that fulfilled their highest expectations for my personal happiness, the definition of which was still evolving.

One day, after my father and I had lunched together on potato salad sandwiches that my mother had brought from home (she was careful about keeping the salad and bread separate until the last moment before we were ready to eat so that the bread wouldn't become soggy), my father asked me, "Would you ever want to be a CEO?"

I laughed. I thought that was a funny question. It reminded me of the time my little cousin Galen, then twelve or thirteen years old, announced to all the parents, "I want to grow up to be a CEO." Then, "What's a CEO?"

"No." I shook my head, lowering my head and biting into my sandwich.

"Why not?" my father asked.

"Daddy! You know why not!"

"No. No, I don't. You've never told me." Often, I've come to realize, the biggest truths we know about ourselves are the things we don't bother saying out loud. We take for granted that everyone already knows.

"I'm not a leader," I said. "I think I work best alone."

My father considered this, chewing slowly. "That's disappointing!" He laughed good-naturedly.

Later, when we were packing up to go home, my father said to me, "Maybe one day, you could write about me." I looked at him, then past him. I saw on his bookshelf the photograph of my mother, my brother, and me that we had taken when the three of us had lived in San Francisco and my father had lived in Taiwan, working hard to get the company started. My mother had taken us shopping at Safeway, and the three of us had squeezed into a Photo-me booth and closed the dirty orange curtains. She had told us to smile big for my father, who missed us terribly in Taiwan. I could see our reflection in the window that covered the camera. My brother was standing on the stool behind my mother, slouched over her right shoulder, and my mother was holding me with one arm on her lap. In the window, I could see the excitement in all of our eyes. My mother looked so pretty with her delicate, upside-down-7 nose and pink lips. Alex looked goofy, smiling with both rows of teeth showing and his eyes barely even opened. I didn't have my two front teeth yet, so I had curled up my tongue to cover my missing teeth. My mother said "cheese," and the flash went off. We mailed my father the picture, and it has since stayed in his office.

"Yes," I said, "maybe."

It didn't take long for Billy and me to fall into a routine. He worked from nine to five at the law firm, reading over government contracts. When there wasn't enough work for him to do, he began bringing books to the office, finishing *Ulysses,* then *To the Lighthouse,* which he had found on the bookshelves in our old Taipei apartment. We usually met in the city after work and had dinner, and then I would have to catch the ten o'clock metro back to my parents' apartment in Tamsui. On the weekends, we watched movies or went out with our friends. We were saving our trip around the island for the end of the summer. It all felt terribly normal and mundane at the time. It rarely occurred to me to be in awe of the fact that Billy was living and working in Taiwan, that he was living in the apartment where I had grown up, sleeping on my brother's bottom bunk, on the same, now completely washed-out, tan sheets that my brother had used throughout high school. I rarely stopped myself short to marvel that he was eating shaved ice at my favorite roadside stand in a back alley in downtown Taipei or that he was buying drinks from the bar where my friends and I had bought our first vodka shots when we were freshmen in high school. But then one night, when Alex was in Taipei for the weekend and we had gone to one of his friends' birthday parties at a bar, Billy sat back on the couch (after he had lost a Taiwanese drinking game to my brother) and said quietly to me, "I could live here." He was smiling and holding my hand and rubbing the back of it with his thumb. And that's when I realized that the normalcy of our summer in Taipei was precisely what was so amazing about it. I wasn't as surprised at Billy's being in Taiwan as I had prepared myself to be because, against the backdrop of my home, Billy fit right in. He was at home, in Taiwan.

When I think of it now, I can't stop marveling at how easily Billy fit into my life at home, despite my mother's uneasiness with him. He made it so effortless for me to show him the side of me that I had, until then, guarded from people I have made friends with since leaving home. Whatever rupture there was between my identity from before I had left Taiwan and the one I had forged after leaving Taiwan was joined in one coherent story by Billy's understanding. He witnessed not only the Taiwaneseness of where I had grown up but also the specific details that had made up my childhood. Like the pirate treasure burial ground of his youth in San Diego, I now had similar memories I could let him in on—memories in places that he didn't have to imagine to see but could see and imagine. He now knew what my childhood room looked like and could imagine the time when my girlfriends had been over and the magazine picture of Jackie Cheung I had taped to my closet door had fallen over and revealed the then-long-haired Michael Bolton on the back and how that had sent us off laughing, clutching our stomachs. We visited my school together, and he could see me walking and talking with my best friend, Kate, taking our sweet old time to do the one-mile run for P.E. One afternoon, while talking in my room, Billy opened up my drawer, and we found a pack of Marlboro Lights (with the surgeon general's warning printed in Chinese), so old that the otherwise-empty drawer was littered with flecks of loosened tobacco. I told him about the first few times I'd smoked in high school and how, because my parents were often not home, my friends would ask to stash their cigarettes in my drawers.

I think while we were in Taiwan that summer, I took Billy's adaptability for granted because it wasn't until we had come back to the States that I began to be surprised. It wasn't until we had developed all the pictures that he'd taken (on all our travels, Billy photographs, and I write) and I saw my home through his eyes that I realized what our summer in Taiwan had meant to him, and to me. On weeknights during the summer when I had to catch the ten o'clock metro back to my parents' or on days when I ran errands with my mother, Billy would walk around the city with his camera and photograph all the things that were to me just part of a larger, blurrier idea of home. He photographed the apartment building that I had grown up in—something that my family had never thought to do because we all knew what that seven-story, black-tiled building looked like. When giving directions to visiting guests, my mother used to tell them they'd recognize our building because it was that "ugly little one right next to the bank." Billy photographed my childhood home from an angle that showed its clear outline against the sky, and behind it, one could see the scalloped rooftop of another building, one built in the traditional Chinese architectural style. He took pictures of sunsets at Chiang Kai-shek memorial, where my father had taken me to ride my pink bike and promised that my training wheels would lift off from the ground. There was a photograph of Kuan-yin Mountain taken from a moving car on his way into Tamsui, the pinks and lavenders of the sky blending softly together like a Chinese painting.

And then there were the photographs that Billy had taken on our week-long trip around the island at the end of the summer: Photographs of red-pillared temples in Tainan; the beaches in Kenting, where my class had gone for our senior class trip and my friends and I had rented mopeds and I had gotten into an accident, permanently scarring the skin around my ankle; the rushing waterfalls in Taroko Gorge, and the luscious, aqua color of the ocean seen from Green Island, a tiny island off the eastern coast of Taiwan. Even though I had always felt that Taiwan was, indeed, Ilha Formosa, "beautiful island," as Portuguese navigators called it in the 1600s, I had never known it with as much conviction and emotion as I did when I looked at Billy's photographs of my home.

I realized that until our summer in Taiwan, I had also been taking home for granted. Until I shared Taiwan with Billy, home was just a collection of ready-made memories, and I was separated from home the same way two magnets with like charges repel each other. But seeing the loving way that Billy had photographed Taiwan, and remembering the eager way he had experienced Taiwan and how he had told me that he could live here, I began to unravel my own prejudice against home. I began to feel that I, too, could live there.

We realized that we could live in Taiwan, but we had come to this realization with a deep-seated understanding that it would not always be easy and effortless, the rose-tinted way in which I was already beginning to remember our trip. When we returned to Taipei after our travels around the island, we had only a few more days before flying back to New York. My parents wanted to take us out to a nice dinner at a French restaurant. Billy and I arrived at the restaurant first. The restaurant was much fancier than I had expected—for the four of us, my parents had reserved a small private room looking out into the small back garden—and Billy was upset at me for not telling him to dress more appropriately. He was wearing a heather-gray, collared, short-sleeve shirt; I reassured him that he looked just fine. The maitre d' who had shown us to our table now quietly excused himself and scooted backward out of our room, closing the door. Billy and I sat at the table, looking around. There was a large pot of orchids in one corner of the room; in another corner, a slim closet of wines slanted downward at a forty-five-degree angle. The air conditioner whirred. Billy nervously played with the tines of his fork, pressing the pads of his fingers into their points. I reached over and squeezed his hand and told him again that he looked fine. I was also afraid that my mother would come in now, catch him playing with his fork, and silently accuse him of having bad manners, proving to herself that we should not be together.

The door opened again, and we saw the maitre d' extend his arm into the room as my mother and father walked in. My mother was wearing a powder-pink qi-pao top with a matching skirt and handbag, all tailor-made from the same material. My father was wearing a white shirt with a stand collar and a black jacket. Billy smoothed the front of his shirt with his hands as he stood up to greet them.

At dinner, we talked about our trip around Taiwan and then about going back to the States, where both Billy and I would begin our second years in graduate school. My father made jokes, and I responded enthusiastically, wanting to compensate for Billy and my mother's relative subdued dispositions. Whenever our door opened and the waiter came in to tell us the specials, take our order, or pour our wine, we paused our conversation and intermittently smiled down at our plates or up at our waiter. I would look at Billy; my father, at my mother.

Just as we were about to begin our main course, the waiter came into our room again and stood by my father's chair and whispered something in his ear. My father took his napkin out of his lap and pushed himself back from the table.

"I think a friend of mine is eating outside in the main dining room. I'm going to go say hello. I'll be right back." I watched my father leave the room with a yearning for him to return as quickly as possible. My mother told us we didn't have to wait for my father to begin eating; we shouldn't let our food get cold. But as I picked up my fork and knife, my mother made no move to begin eating. No one talked as Billy and I cut into our food. The *tink tink* of our utensils tapping against the ceramic plates were the only sounds in the room. We brought cut-up pieces of food to our mouths gingerly and chewed self-consciously as my mother watched us, still not touching her food. Billy complimented his duck and thanked my mother for her earlier recommendation. My mother smiled and then looked down. Now she began playing with the tines of her fork. She opened her mouth and sucked in some air as if she were going to say something, but then closed her mouth again. She began to draw small circles on the white tablecloth with her index finger. She opened her mouth again, but this time, she began what she had planned to say.

"You know," she said, looking up at Billy. Even before she continued, I knew my mother wanted to tell Billy how his presence in our family made her feel. I knew that she was going to tell him how "uncomfortable" she was about our relationship. I knew that she had been waiting for this moment when my father wouldn't be around to protect us and admonish her as she unloaded the burden of her prejudice on us. I wanted to say something to stop her, but nothing came out. I looked at the back of Billy's head because it was turned toward my mother, and wondered whether he knew what was coming. My mother continued to speak.

"You know, I'm not as open-minded as Brenda's father is. I have felt—"

At that very moment, the door to our room swung open, and my father bounded in with his friend in tow, laughing loudly, oblivious to what he had just interrupted, saying, "Look who's here!"

Billy turned his attention to my father and his friend, and I watched as my mother's mouth—opened, in mid-sentence—closed slowly and hesitantly.

She looked at my father standing in the door frame and smiled coldly. The timing of it all felt impossibly perfect, like a ridiculous comedy. There was my father again, rescuing us from my mother. I saw Billy's shoulders relax, and we smiled at each other. He knew precisely what was going on. I almost felt sorry for my mother when she had to get up from her chair and say hello to my father's friend and pretend that nothing had happened.

After dinner, I went home with my parents, and Billy caught the bus back to the Taipei apartment. We said good-bye without our usual lingering hug and kiss, and I told him that I would call him when I got home. Sitting in the back seat of my father's car, I was reminded of the countless drives home from dinner parties with my parents. Usually, my brother and I would look out our windows at passing trees and buildings as my parents talked in low voices in the front. They would talk about adult things—their life without us, in which I was always interested because they suddenly became people other than my parents, people with their own concerns, concerns that did not include me—and sometimes conversed in Japanese when there was something they didn't want us to hear. That rarely worked because I could often understand from context. Later, my father would turn on the radio to the classical music station—his favorite show was hosted by a German-Taiwanese couple who played duets on the piano and introduced classical music, all in a soft, close tone, all in Chinese—and I would eventually fall asleep, my temple resting on the coolness of the window.

Ten minutes into our drive to Tamsui, it started to drizzle, and I watched the water globules on the window turn red, green, and yellow as we passed brightly lit neon signs.

"I don't know," my mother suddenly said to my father in Taiwanese.

"Don't know what?"

"I don't know why I have been feeling so uncomfortable these days. Like there's something weighing down on me." My father was silent; he kept his eyes on the road. I couldn't tell whether my mother thought I couldn't hear them talking or if she was also indirectly talking to me. Either way, it was clear she wanted a second chance to say what she had been unable to finish at the restaurant.

My father groaned quietly. He turned his head and looked at my mother, who was looking out the window. "Mommy," he said with a mixture of affection and mild annoyance, "I know what's 'weighing down' on you."

"You do?" She looked at my father.

"Yes, but I don't want to talk about it now. Not here." I saw my father's neck stretch a little as he tried to look at me in the rearview mirror. I looked out the window.

When we arrived at home, my parents headed straight to their bedroom, and I to mine; we did not say good-night. Without changing, I dropped onto my futon mattress on the floor and lay on my stomach, my face pressing hard into my pillow, where I could smell the faded scent of my mother's perfume.

TRANSLATIONS

On September 20, 1999, as Taichung Ah-ma (my mother's mother) was reaching for something in the upstairs bathroom in her San Francisco house, she felt an excruciating pain shoot all up and down her back. It hurt so much that she crumpled onto the cold, pink tiles and tried to wait for the pain to subside. Luckily, her son Joe had just stopped by to drop off that morning's Taiwanese paper. When he hello-ed into the house and heard only a faint whimper come from the bathroom, he rushed up the carpeted stairs and found his mother in a helpless heap on the floor. He took her to the hospital. One of the discs in her vertebrae had slipped, no longer providing the soft cushioning between two of her backbones. The bones grated against each other, the pain radiating from the small of her back.

On the same day, there was a massive earthquake in Taiwan that measured 7.6 on the Richter scale. The epicenter was at Nantou, a county just a few kilometers away from my grandmother's ophthalmology clinic in Taichung. Above the clinic was the house in which my mother had grown up with her three sisters and younger brother—the house that my grandfather had designed. Fortunately, the house did not suffer any severe damages. But my mother's younger sister, Ally, lived closer to the fault, and the ground under her house ruptured and pushed the one-story house up to a two-story height. Taichung Ah-ma believed that the slipped discs in her vertebrae were a direct effect of the chafing plates under the earth's lithosphere at Nantou.

On the day of the earthquake, I was at school, researching a piece I wanted to write on two-two-eight. I did not learn about the earthquake until 6 p.m.; it had started at 1:47 a.m. Taiwan time (1:47 p.m. in New York), about the time I had begun my research in the library. At dusk, I was wrapping up my Internet research and logged onto a news site, where the headlines screamed, *Trembler hits Taiwan, Quake of the century, Thousands dead, hundreds still missing!* I ran out of the library, disoriented. People on the sidewalk swished by, blurring, suddenly looking like extras in the background of a movie scene. I had just moved into my apartment in New York and did not yet have a phone connected. With sudden clarity, I rushed toward the nearest newspaper vendor and bought a phone card to call my parents in Taiwan. I used a telephone on the corner of 112th and Broadway, pressing the phone tightly against my left ear, jamming my right finger into the other ear. There was a loud, hollow noise after I dialed our number at home. A few seconds later, I could hear the faint, delayed repetition of the tones of our telephone number. Then—"We're sorry," a recording said to me, deadpan and unsympathetic, "we cannot connect you with the country you wish to call at this moment."

I ran back to my apartment on 89th Street, trying phones on every other corner. The one time I did get through, there was no answer. I imagined hearing the hollow ring of the telephone through our empty apartment in Tamsui. I wondered whether the antique porcelain vases and Buddhist figurines my mother had collected over the past thirty years had fallen during the earthquake. I called my aunt in Queens and asked whether she had heard from my parents. She hadn't. But I should keep calling back to check, she told me.

Finally, I got through to my parents the next day. They had been asleep when they were shaken out of bed. They had scrambled into the dining room and hid under the large, round wooden table. There, they had held onto each other closely, their bodies swaying with the shaking earth as they looked into one another's fearful eyes. Eventually, they got used to the sound of shattering china as my mother's antiques fell, one by one, from the display shelves in the living room. They were still experiencing aftershocks, my father told me. When he handed the phone over to my mother, she described what she had seen that morning, walking on the streets outside: There were arms and legs sticking out from underneath the rubble—her voice cracked, and I *shhh*ed into the telephone.

Where my grandmother, my mother, and I were on the day of the earthquake was, to me, a mapping of the way we have each come to relate to Taiwan: Though Taichung Ah-ma was in the San Francisco house that she and my grandfather moved into more than twenty years before, she still felt a deep and spiritual connection with Taiwan, believing that her back suffered from slipped discs because of the earthquake in Taiwan. I was in graduate school in New York, connecting myself to home from a distance, delving deep into my relationship with Taiwan by studying its history. And my mother, who, after four years' living in America in the 1970s, had decided with my father to move back to Taiwan when everyone else was emigrating to the United States, was there when the first tremors were felt throughout the island. The three of us represented the three generations of our specific Taiwanese history—my grandmother was born in 1919, right in the middle of the Japanese occupation; my mother in 1944, just three years before the February 28th Incident when islanders began asking what it meant to be Taiwanese; and I was born in 1976 in San Francisco, just as the United States cut off relations with the island to favor its ties with Mainland China.

My mother had come to the same conclusion about our relationships to Taiwan long before the earthquake hit the island in September and had expressed her desire to collaborate with Taichung Ah-ma and me on a project that would translate this idea into a literary form. At the time, she was working on a book on her collection of cloth baby carriers from aboriginal tribes in China. She was fascinated by the intricacies and handiwork of these carriers that young mothers would make for their newborn babies. Her idea was that, interspersed between the texts, which described and explained the meaning behind repeated motifs in the baby carriers and the traditions involved in making them, would be essays written by my grandmother, herself, and me on mothers and motherhood. And because all three of us had grown up in Taiwan, we were to use Taiwan as the common background in our essays. Each of us was instructed to write in what has become our native tongue—Japanese for Taichung Ah-ma, Chinese for my mother, and English for me—and then my mother would translate the Japanese and English pieces into Chinese so that my grandmother and I could read and translate one another's pieces since neither of us spoke the other's language fluently. My mother would essentially be the literary liaison between Taichung Ah-ma and me. Through our translations, our book would show how three Taiwanese women talked to each other across generations and cultures.

Whether or not she had intended it, my mother's project had opened up a channel through which the two of us, in particular, could have the dialogues that we rarely had in conversation. Where there was silence and even a sense of discomfort when the two of us talked, our essays and translations of one another's writings proved that we understood each other in a more profound way than we were capable of showing. We did not have the faculties to talk openly with each other—our shared Taiwanese culture did not teach us how, and my "American" desire to break down that silence made both of us uncomfortable. But through writing, we found the privacy we both needed to be candid. We weren't just translating languages—we were translating emotions.

In the January after the earthquake, after we'd spent Christmas and New Year's separately, Taichung Ah-ma, my mother, and I convened in Ah-ma's house in San Francisco. We were there to begin work on our book, but because of Ah-ma's worsening back condition, my mother and I ended up spending most of our time helping my grandmother around the house. It was the first time I remember seeing my mother cook in Taichung Ah-ma's kitchen. Ah-ma could stand upright for only twenty minutes at a time. Most of the day, she lay in the small wooden bed in my grandfather's study upstairs. She had begun sleeping there when he had died three years before, saying that she liked to be close to him by being close to his books. My mother brought her a whole stack of Japanese books so she could read in bed.

Every day, my mother and I would run various errands—we went grocery shopping and straightened up the house, and when Ah-ma needed something, she would jingle an antique iron bell that she kept by her side, and I would run up the stairs. Usually, she needed a glass of water or she would ask me to rub the small of her back where it was sore. She always asked me to do things for her shyly, unaccustomed to being the one to ask for help because she was the one who had taken care of my grandfather in the last years that he was alive. A few times, my mother and I brought up one of my grandfather's paintings from his studio in the basement and held it in the doorway for my grandmother to look at as she lay in his bed. My grandfather had done mostly landscape and figure paintings—using lively compositions and bold color combinations. (One that the three of us especially liked was a portrait of a girl in a red dress with her arm in a green-tinted shadow.) My grandfather had emulated the German Expressionists, wanting to rebel against the rigidity and emphasis on conventional technique that his art education in Taiwan had taught. After the three of us talked about his paintings, we would talk about my grandfather. He and my grandmother had been married for almost sixty years, and she missed him terribly.

At night, we gathered around Taichung Ah-ma on her bed. We sat up against the wall and stuck our feet underneath the covers, wriggling our toes to keep warm. We sat and talked and giggled like girls at a slumber party. The conversations were mostly in Taiwanese for my benefit, since my mother was fluent in Japanese.

One night, my grandmother started asking me about Billy. She had met him briefly when he had driven me up from San Diego to her house a day before my mother arrived. She had stood by the door when Billy and I smiled at each other and waved good-bye, wanting to hold each other but respecting that for my grandmother, physical contact was reserved for family and private moments. After we had closed the door, Taichung Ah-ma had turned to me, her gray eyes soft and glistening, her powder white hair in wisps around her face, and said, "You two have something very special. You share a deep connection that I could feel." I had turned to her, my eyes bright and excited. I had wanted to burst out, how did you know that? But instead, I had taken her hand in mine and held her close, rubbing the slight hump in her upper back as I kissed the thin, pink skin on her cheek.

I realized that I was like my grandmother because I had a lot of faith in my intuition. In Mandarin, there is a word for that feeling of knowing, of connecting, when you first meet someone—yuan. It is a sense that you share with the other person. When I met Billy for the first time in St. Petersburg, I knew that the two of us had yuan. In the beginning, this feeling was inexplicable because we hardly knew each other, but the conviction that we had yuan came from my gut, and though I couldn't give concrete reasons to support my feeling, I felt it strongly enough. This was the same way Taichung Ah-ma must have felt about seeing me and Billy together that morning. I remember trying to explain yuan to Billy toward the end of our summer in

Russia. I began by telling him that this was an untranslatable word, to which he furrowed his eyebrows and said he didn't believe there was such a thing; he thought every word had an equivalent in another language. I disagreed. After I explained and described yuan to him, using us as an example, his eyes brightened, and he immediately understood what I was talking about and agreed that he knew, too, that we had yuan. Whenever he referred to it, he always said yuan, and in later conversations, admitted that he had been wrong, that not every word had an equivalent in another language. We finally decided that both the beauty and difficulty in translations was the fact that literal translations were inadequate—one had to understand the nuances of a language and a culture to translate from one language to another and preserve the full sense of a word, a sentence, an idea.

Taichung Ah-ma repeated what she had told me the day she met Billy to my mother that night in her bed. My mother looked perplexed, seeming to ask the same question I had wanted to ask Ah-ma that day, but in a suspicious tone—how could you know that? She didn't say anything and only made a barely audible "mmm" sound in response. Taichung Ah-ma turned to me and said that she knew relationships among people in my generation were completely different from the way things used to be for her and for my mother's generation. My grandfather had been a reporter when he was young, and once he had heard a rumor about a very pretty eye doctor who lived in southern Taiwan. He had made up an assignment to go down south and found Taichung Ah-ma, who was then practicing in a small town. He saw that what he'd heard was true—the lady doctor had a round, soft face and pencil-thin eyebrows with arches just so that the angle lent a certain air of mystery. Soon, my grandfather had fallen in love with Ah-ma's gentle beauty and strong intellect, and the two of them spent time together and were married.

The story, even as Taichung Ah-ma told it, unfolded that simply. Maybe, she pondered, things were easier when people just got married. Now, there were so many factors to consider, so many trial periods one was granted, and one's circle of friends was so much larger and more diverse. She asked me how I thought I could reconcile the generational and cultural differences that my mother and I were bound to have on the subject. I looked straight into my grandmother's eyes, never shifting my gaze as I told her how I believed that my parents and I shared the same set of values (values which they had taught me to have) and how, because of that, I had every faith that the person I chose to love could not possibly be someone they could not come to love, as well. I said this with a terrible consciousness that my mother was watching me and that I was really saying this to her. Taichung Ah-ma turned to my mother and said that she thought I had a very clear head about the matter and turned back to look at me and reminded me that love was never about two people alone, but about families and cultures.

"You know, when Ah-gong, your grandfather, asked me to marry him, my parents were against the idea."

I was surprised. My grandparents had a marriage that all my aunts and uncles, and even Meiguo Ah-ma, respected and envied. They had had an unconventional relationship in which my grandmother supported the family because she was a doctor, and my grandfather went through different jobs before finally becoming a painter. He was a perfectionist who was possessive about his work—once, he had painted a portrait of a painter friend in exchange for a portrait his friend would make of him, but in the end, my grandfather wouldn't give up the portrait he'd painted of his friend because he claimed "it was never finished." But Taichung Ah-ma and Ah-gong had understood and respected one another's needs and were always considerate and supportive with each other. When Ah-gong was still alive, he and Taichung Ah-ma would each tell me separately what a wonderful and intelligent person the other was and how it was so important to find someone like that for a life partner. It was difficult for me to imagine that a couple who had enjoyed almost sixty years of an exceptionally loving marriage had once had trouble convincing others that they shared something extraordinary.

Taichung Ah-ma explained that her parents could not, at first, accept Ah-gong because he was Hakka, a group from the mainland who had never assimilated into the native Chinese culture. In Mandarin, Hakka means guest. When Taichung Ah-ma's family traced their ancestry back to the mainland, they learned that they belonged to the main part of Han Chinese and not a group that had broken off and secluded itself from mainstream Chinese culture like the Hakka. The Hakka were viewed as clannish, peripheral, and even rebellious—they were the first to forbid their women to bind their feet. Taichung Ah-ma's parents were alive at a time when Taiwanese culture was still largely based on its connection to Chinese culture on the mainland. They thought that because my grandfather was Hakka, he was too different and therefore not a good match for my grandmother.

"But we had a deep and mature relationship from the very beginning," my grandmother told me, "and with time, my parents could see that, and they were finally able to accept Ah-gong. Of course, it wasn't always easy. There were many minor differences that we all had to learn how to compromise with each other." Taichung Ah-ma looked quickly at my mother and then me. "Sometimes, the things that are most important to you take a longer time to establish with the people who love you the most."

I didn't ask my grandmother why this was at the time, but when I thought about what she'd said later, I could see how the more someone cared about you, the more he or she would expect from your relationships. It was part of human nature to be possessive and protective over the people we love. This need to shield a loved one against any potential harm was perhaps most pronounced in the love a mother had for her child. It wasn't until Billy and I spent the summer in Taiwan six months later that I experienced this very concept with the way my mother put up a guard against Billy.

"Sometimes," my mother said suddenly, "love can be about politics." Taichung Ah-ma and I turned to look at her. "How does Billy see you? Does he see you as American or Taiwanese?" my mother asked in a challenging tone. My mother was always asking me to choose my allegiance—to her, it was as if the answer were black or white, one or the other, and never something in-between. It was as if my being both Taiwanese and American didn't have anything to do with the choices she and my father had made for my brother and me.

"He sees me the way I see myself," I answered.

"Which is . . . " she pressed.

"Well," I said, "I'm both. I'm American." I looked at my mother hard. "Because you and Daddy made me American and because that's the kind of education I got. But I'm also Taiwanese." I looked down at Taichung Ah-ma, who was smiling slightly, waiting expectantly for the rest of my answer. "I'm also Taiwanese because I grew up there and I've inherited all these values and habits from Mommy and Daddy that I know are uniquely Taiwanese. Plus," I added, "Taiwan will always be the place where I come from. That could never change."

"And Billy understands this?" my mother asked. "He gets all of that and accepts it?"

"Of course," I said firmly. "Otherwise, we wouldn't be together."

"Well," my mother grumbled under her breath and looked away.

"Did you know," Taichung Ah-ma spoke up, "that when your Aunt Nancy and Uncle John wanted to get married, Ah-gong was very upset that his daughter was going to marry a wai guo ren—a foreigner?" Aunt Nancy was one of my mother's younger sisters, the one who had lived with us from time to time in San Francisco when my parents were separated those four years.

"Really?" I was thankful that Taichung Ah-ma was interjecting at all the moments when the conversation between my mother and me were most tense. She seemed to be acting as our liaison, even though linguistically, it was still my mother who was translating the ends of my and Taichung Ah-ma's sentences into Japanese, Taiwanese, or English for us.

My grandmother told me how it had taken Uncle John almost seven years to get my grandfather's approval for their wedding. Inside, she said, Ah-gong had really liked John and thought he was an intelligent and genuine man. Ah-gong was impressed that John was a professor at Caltech and that his science-minded daughter had a companion with whom she could connect both intellectually and emotionally. But he was stubborn and old-fashioned about John's not being Taiwanese, seeming to forget that he had once been in a position similar to John's, when Taichung Ah-ma's parents hadn't approved of him because he was Hakka. Finally, he realized he could no longer stand in the way of his daughter's marriage for such selfish and narrow-minded reasons. On the day when John and Nancy got married, Ah-gong gave them a painting he had made of two fiery red-orange pomegranates against a backdrop of cool, bluish white. That was the first time he had given his painting to someone as a gift.

"It takes time." Taichung Ah-ma finished the story and squeezed my hand.

"I know," I said.

"And now." She laughed, embarrassed. "I think I am tired. I've been lying down all day, and still, I get sleepy!"

My mother and I got up and tucked her into bed, and I kissed Ah-ma good-night. The two of us went into the adjacent room, the room that used to be my grandparents' bedroom, and quietly got ready for bed, too. After we had both slipped into the big, king-sized bed, I lay on my back, blinking my eyes into the darkness, thinking about how much I had to learn from my grandmother and how much more she understood me than I was aware of. I felt my mother shift as she turned her back to me, pulling the sheets over my body toward her side of the bed. I could hear her steady breathing. I knew that she was still awake. I closed my eyes for about twenty minutes, hyper-aware of my own movements next to my mother.

"Are you asleep?" my mother whispered suddenly into the darkness. Her back was still toward me. I opened my eyes and tried to locate the ceiling.

"No."

There was a long moment of silence. She was trying to decide something.

"What's Billy like?" she finally asked.

It was the first time my mother had taken the initiative to ask me about Billy. We both relaxed; I could feel our bodies sink into the bed with some ease. Then we stayed up for half an hour more, and I told her about Billy.

The next day after breakfast, while Taichung Ah-ma was upstairs reading, my mother and I went into the dining room downstairs, where Ah-ma had set a framed photograph of Ah-gong on a table in front of which she kept a ceramic bowl of ashes for burning incense and a small pot of fresh flowers. My mother pulled out a clear plastic folder of her notes on the baby carriers. There were photographs of each carrier taped to some of the sheets of paper. Around the photographs crawled my mother's small and delicate Chinese script in blue and black ink, alternating arbitrarily because she wrote with whatever pen she happened to find on her desk. She wanted to explain her notes to me verbally so that she knew I understood how best to translate her written texts on the baby carriers. The first thing we went over together was my mother's preface to the book, where she explains her connection to aboriginal baby carriers.

My mother had always been a collector of Chinese antiques. For the past ten years, she had worked as a volunteer tour guide at the National Palace Museum in Taipei, and whenever she and my father came to New York, we always made a trip to the Metropolitan Museum. In the dark, lonely rooms of the East Asian wing, my mother would walk us through the collections of ceramics and bronzes. She could stand a few feet from a blue and white ceramic pot and tell us which dynasty it was from, how the dyes were mixed, and the approximate year it was made. My father and I would run up ahead of her and check the small card in front of the pot to find that she would be right every time. After working at my father's children's clothing company for thirty years, my mother had retired and was spending her time pursuing her real passion: researching, collecting, and writing about Chinese art. While I was growing up, I had often seen my mother bent over big art books on Sunday afternoons, her reading glasses slipping halfway down her straight, narrow nose, a pen in one hand and a tape recorder on one corner of her desk. Sometimes she spoke her notes into the recorder; other times, she played tapes of university art lectures. I had always admired her steadfastness in her passion for art. She taught me what a blessing it was to have a passion, to really be in love with what you do. You will always be happy, she had told me, as long as you follow your passions—that is how one attains success.

Recently, in addition to her collection of Chinese antiques, my mother began a collection of folk art from aboriginal tribes (minority groups) in China. She was in an antique shop in Hong Kong a few years back when she stumbled upon a rectangular piece of cloth, elaborately designed and brilliantly dyed. She looked closely and found repeating patterns of little bats all along the border of the cloth. She asked the shop owner what she was holding, and he told her that it was a baby carrier from the Miao tribe in southern China. "Bat" in Chinese, is fu, a close homonym of the word for luck. The young mothers of the Miao tribe used motifs like this one in all their baby carriers, the shop owner explained to my mother; they put all their wishes for their newborn babies' futures and good fortune into the design of these carriers. My mother already had a collection of children's hats from nineteenth-century China—some were sewn in the shapes of tigers, dragons, and other auspicious animals; others were decorated with symbols like the bat—a way for mothers to wish their children good luck. She had written a book on these hats two years before and was not unfamiliar with the emotions involved with the process of making and designing these children's garments. Moreover, what my mother did now was not so different from the career she had shared with my father for thirty years, designing children's clothing.

But as my mother held that baby carrier in her hands that day in Hong Kong, she was confused about one thing. How did the mother carry her baby with just a rectangular piece of cloth? The shop owner told her that what she was holding was only a part of the baby carrier. Usually, there were two broad strips of cloth—sometimes in the same design, other times in contrasting color and design—that were attached to the main piece, and the mother would tie these ribbons tightly around her waist so that her baby fit snugly against her chest or on her back with the main piece of cloth covering the baby's back. When the mothers sold their old baby carriers, they would cut off these ties and sell only the square or rectangular piece of cloth in the middle. The ties were like the umbilical cords that connected a mother to her child when a baby was born. These mothers did not ever want to part with this physical representation of their bond with their children. When my mother heard this, she was immediately fascinated by the idea of an umbilical cord that a mother could keep.

On my parents' twentieth anniversary, my mother had written a short essay in Chinese that she shared with family and friends entitled, "Wealth Ribbon." It was one of the pieces that she wanted to include in our book, which I later translated. The piece begins:

> Before I was married, Mother handed me an envelope. Inside, I found the umbilical cord that had dried up and fallen off a few days after I was born. Mother said this was for me to keep from now on. On the yellowed traditional-style envelope, Father had written—with his elegant Chinese calligraphy—the time and date I was born and noted that this was "Christi's wealth ribbon."

In Taiwanese, "wealth ribbon" and "umbilical cord" are homonyms. In addition to saving my umbilical cord in remembrance of my once-physical tie to my mother, Father also wanted to wish me a life of wealth and happiness.

I didn't remember reading this piece ten years ago on my parents' anniversary, and even if I had, I don't think I was old enough to understand the profound implications of Taichung Ah-ma and Ah-gong's gift to my mother and my mother's deep appreciation of her parents' blessings. Reading this piece as all the photographs of my mother's baby carriers were spread across my grandparents' dining table, I could suddenly tie together all the different parts that made up this project on which my grandmother, my mother, and I were collaborating. The umbilical cord that my grandmother had given my mother represented the same things that Miao baby carriers represented—they were both a reminder of that physical bond between mother and child and a channel through which a mother could bestow blessings on her child.

In the context of our project, I also began to see how the relationship between a mother and her daughter was especially unique and precious, for women in Chinese families shared the same outsider identity. A daughter was always married out of her family and into her husband's. That's why in Mandarin, Taichung Ah-ma was my wai po, my "grandmother from outside." When Billy and I had been in Taiwan for four days before our China trip, we had happened to fly in on the weekend of Tomb Sweeping Day, a national holiday in the spring when families visit their ancestors' graves, sweeping clean the little plot of cement ground in front of the headstones and putting fresh flowers in the stone vases before the graves. This was a tradition my family had kept when I was growing up—we visited my father's father and Meiguo Ah-ma's mother's tombs, but never the graves of my mother's ancestors. Our family would stand in front of the graves with our heads bowed. Meiguo Ah-ma and my father would mumble something under their breaths—all I could ever make out in their whispers was the Taiwanese word for "thankful," gam xia. Then, we would watch for the cue from Meiguo Ah-ma after she had finished her prayer—when she bowed, we bowed, and when she lifted her head, we lifted our heads. We always bowed three times. When Meiguo Ah-ma wasn't in Taiwan for Tomb Sweeping Day, it was my father's cue that we followed.

A few years ago, our family moved my grandfather and great-grandmother to a bigger site, to a small mausoleum atop a mountain, next to a Buddhist temple. We had dug up the old graves (and found my grandfather's wedding ring still intact, encircling a thin, ivory bone), cremated the remains, and put the ashes in ceramic urns that were placed in a closet behind the large headstones. On Tomb Sweeping Day the year Billy and I were there, my father walked us behind the headstones and showed us a metal door with a lock on it. He pointed to it and told Billy that inside was where we kept the urns and that this was where he, my mother, and my brother would rest after they'd died. "But what about Brenda?" Billy had asked. I hadn't even noticed that my father had left me out of the arrangement.

My mother answered quietly, "She'll be buried with her husband's family."

So my brother would always be my mother's son, but I would eventually become someone else's daughter. This was why the bond between mother and daughter was especially poignant. Taichung Ah-ma, my mother, and I clung to each other because we were all outsiders to our families. In adopting a new family, we had to give up our original one. No one could better understand this lot than one's own mother. The cut umbilical cord, then, as a symbol of the connection between a mother and her child was even more meaningful when it was the umbilical cord between mother and daughter.

Now, as we sat at the dining table in Taichung Ah-ma's house, working together on this book about baby carriers, it was clearer to me than it had ever been before how inextricably tied to my mother I was, and how, in her gesture of asking me to translate her book, she was reestablishing our tie and relating to me not only as mother to daughter, but also as one woman to another.

We had talked the whole morning, and my mother soon noticed that it was time for lunch. She asked me to wash some vegetables as she clicked on the rice cooker. She started to cut up ginger and chicken to make a sesame rice wine soup that was good for cold weather. As she did this, I took notes on a telephone pad, realizing that I had never been in the kitchen with my mother and had never asked her to teach me how to cook. Whenever she hosted dinner parties at our house, she would be in the kitchen all day, even throughout dinner, and never asked any of us to help her. Now I watched her stir-fry cabbage and carrots and panfry a filet of salmon. My mother moved with a steady assuredness that reminded me of the way I'd pictured her those years when she had lived in San Francisco without my father. She instructed me to make a salad and dice some Fuji apples in it, a touch that we'd learned from Taichung Ah-ma. When we finished putting lunch together, I went upstairs, helped Taichung Ah-ma out of bed, and walked her slowly down the stairs. The three of us sat at the kitchen table—a simple wooden rectangle with two long, skinny benches on either side, which were Chinese antiques that my grandfather had collected when he was young—and ate to the ticking of a clock made out of a ceramic plate, all the numbers replaced by the backwards E's on eye charts, a remnant of Taichung Ah-ma's clinic back in Taiwan.

When I was in Taiwan with Billy later that year, my grandmother was spending most of her summer in Taichung at her old clinic, where her daughter Ally was now also a practicing ophthalmologist. Ah-ma was eighty-two, but she still saw patients when my Aunt Ally was too busy. In the clinic, there was a small back room sectioned off by a thin curtain where Taichung Ah-ma would use acupuncture to help some of her patients who came in for more than just optical problems—a young boy who had lost his appetite, a woman who felt as though she had not slept for ten years. In her dark acupuncture room, Taichung Ah-ma talked with these patients as she gently stuck long, thin needles into their pressure points. They came back days later, thanking my grandmother with baskets of fruit and flowers. When Taichung Ah-ma had been a young doctor, many of her patients who hadn't had money to pay for their treatment would bring her vegetables from their gardens instead. My mother wrote about this later in an essay about her mother.

When Taichung Ah-ma wasn't doing work around the clinic, she sat down in a study upstairs and wrote her essays for our baby carrier book. Meanwhile, I did my writing when I had a break from working at my father's office. By July, my grandmother and I had finished writing our pieces for the book and were ready to read and translate one another's essays. My mother had not begun her writing. She told me she didn't know what to write.

"But that's impossible," I said. "This book was your idea. You knew what to write the moment you picked up that baby carrier."

My mother considered this for a while, then replied, "I know, you're right. I do know what to write, but I think I'm just nervous that I can't do this—that I can't write the way I imagine myself writing. Does that ever happen to you?"

"All the time!" I laughed. I had rarely seen my mother so unsure of herself; her insecurity endeared her to me. "Reading helps," I told her. So my mother read all three of Taichung Ah-ma's essays and translated them into Chinese.

My grandmother's pieces were difficult for me to translate into English. One reason was that I was working with a Chinese translation of a Japanese essay. But the other, more significant, reason was that my grandmother's prose read like poetry. When I was studying Russian in college, I had taken a Russian poetry class, and one of our weekly assignments was to translate Mandelshtam, Akhmatova, or Blok's work into English. I found that it was the process of translating that was wonderful—discovering and explicating all the multiplicity of meanings of words—but it was the result of the translation that proved horrendous and barely readable as poetry. I was embarrassed by my translation of Taichung Ah-ma's words but was captivated by the experience of translating her work. Taichung Ah-ma wrote about her mother and her grandmother but wrote about them by writing about place. She described the architecture of her childhood home in Tamsui (the town where my parents lived now), bringing me with her on a day after school from the front door into the deep center of the house—the open courtyard where all the women of the family got together to wash clothes, dry tea leaves, and talk. Taichung Ah-ma grew up in a Taiwan where she did her homework with the window open, the scent of jasmine wafting into her room; where her entire family, including grandparents, aunts, uncles, and cousins, ate together every night, shoulder to shoulder at a round table.

After my mother read Taichung Ah-ma's pieces, she proceeded to write a piece on her mother and, in the same way that Ah-ma had, was able to evoke a concrete sense of place, of Taiwan. Betelnut palms, rice paddies, and courtyard homes were a part of the architecture of their childhood memories. The backdrop of my childhood memories consisted of scaffolding, empty lots, uprooted trees after severe typhoons, then later, skyscrapers, billboards, and neon lights. The increasing modernity of my Taiwan seemed to pale compared to the nostalgia of my mother and grandmother's Taiwan, though I see now how the stark differences in our childhood landscapes are meant to illustrate the passage of time and of generations on our small island.

My mother read my three pieces when she was ready to write her next essay. One of the pieces was a letter I had written to the child I would have in the future. I was inspired to write from the point of view of a mother after I had thought, for a long time, about the source of my mother's resistance to my being with Billy. After our first argument at the beginning of the summer when my father had interjected and "revealed" that my mother couldn't accept Billy's not being Taiwanese, I had been careful about showing my resentment toward my mother whenever she made me feel guilty about my relationship. Any more conflict I had with my mother—however little it really had to do with Billy—would only cast a bad light on what Billy and I shared. Moreover, it had become clear to me that what bothered my mother was more than Billy's not being Taiwanese—his not being able to speak the language, or know, right away, the customs, or be able to recite the history. These were all minor details that we could change (I recalled that when I had had a Taiwanese boyfriend for two years in college, my mother had been equally guarded against him.) In fact, learning the language, the customs, and the history of Taiwan were all efforts that Billy had already voluntarily begun to undertake. I had never asked him to do these things for me, and when I had reassured him that these were not things I expected of him, he shrugged his shoulders and said, "I know. I'm learning these things for me."

I finally concluded that my mother was guarded against Billy because she wanted to protect me from any potential harm I might suffer in life—and especially in love. Ever since I was little, my mother had warned me against boys. After all, she must have thought, it was going to be a boy who would pluck me out of my family and claim me as his family's. One night, when she was tucking me into bed—I was about nine years old—she had said to me as she gently brushed her palm against my forehead, pushing my hair back, "You have to be careful with boys. I know you—you are too easily moved and gullible. Someone will come one day and cheat you out of your feelings."

It's a wonder that what my mother had told me that night did not become a self-fulfilling prophecy. What she'd predicted about me wasn't— and never has been—true. I think, in large part, it was because she was also adamant about teaching me to love and respect myself before I loved another person. "You come first," she used to say, and told me to "dream big dreams" and that I could do whatever I wanted to, as long as I had the will and the imagination for it. There were fewer lessons on relationships, though she did try to teach me by example. She would tell me that I should aspire to a marriage like hers—that it was important to find someone as dependable, intelligent, and humorous as my father. She told me that even though she and my father were not accustomed to saying, "I love you" to each other, as Americans did so easily and frequently, my father showed her he loved her in different ways, every day. Sometimes, he would tell her she was beautiful; other times, he would brag about my mother's artistic sensibility to his friends at a dinner party; but always, my mother told me, my father showed her he loved her because he supported all her interests and gave her her space. Without him, she never could have published her first book on children's hats. But my mother never told me how to go about finding someone like that, and when I went off on my own, she was upset; she felt she had lost control over me or that she didn't understand me any longer. But I think it was, in many ways, my mother who had led me to my relationship with Billy, who was also dependable, intelligent, and humorous, and who also showed me he loved me every day in different ways. In my letter to my future child I wrote:

> I will tell you now that there will be times when I may want to protect you when I know I should trust you and let you go. You must understand that anything I do for you comes only from the deepest part of my love for you—you, who will come from my womb, who will forever be a very real and physical part of me. I know I will desperately wish there were some way I could

guarantee and secure your future happiness, and sometimes, this may translate the wrong way. Know that in the end, it will be your wishes I will respect, but you must allow me to indulge in the kind of possessiveness to which only a mother is entitled.

Isn't it extraordinary that, even though at this moment, I am not yet ready for your arrival, I am already so enthralled and in love with your existence? That, as well, is something I have learned from my mother.

The letter was addressed to my future child, but it was also a letter to my mother. I wanted to tell her that I understood why there had been so much tension between us that summer and what was so difficult about our having open conversations. The truth was, my mother and I functioned on the same plane—neither of us was very good with spoken words and emotions. We fumbled when it came time to articulate our feelings—I often cried, and she often stopped short and turned away. But I realized I could have meaningful conversations with my mother without having to say a word—we could write to each other. In fact, it was my mother who had come up with this idea; it was she who had invited me to talk with her through the written word. Through my translations of her work, and hers of mine, we began opening up to each other. It felt like that night when we had lain on the bed in Taichung Ah-ma's house and it was dark and we weren't looking at each other, but I could feel our bodies ease into the mattress as we slowly started speaking to each other with less reservation, less judgment. After reading my "letter," my mother wrote a piece she titled, "Hope," which I translated:

> Child, before receiving you into my life, neither my pregnancy nor my delivery went very smoothly. But I will always remember when the doctor handed you over to me and I encircled my arms around you—it was a moment of pure joy and satisfaction. All the pain that I had suffered was easily put behind me and quickly forgotten.
>
> From being that helpless baby to the independent woman you are today, we have always been carefully protecting you, observing you, and guiding you along the way. In fact, these

twenty-some years have not all been easy—there have been so many times when, because of our lack of experience or our own naiveté, we did not do the best we could to parent you. But you must believe our sincerity every time we ask the gods to grant us greater wisdom to know how best to allow you to finish becoming who you are meant to be.

We've known for a long time that your life does not belong to us and have come to accept that you are like a fiery arrow and we are but the bow upon which you temporarily rest. But at this moment before you fly out far away from us, we hope that you will love yourself first before you reach out to love others. We also hope that you will always be humble and that you will never stop using your imagination. . . . This is a journey that is all your own, a world that belongs to you.

"Hope" was a letter my mother had written to me, but I believe it was a letter she had written to herself too. The most difficult part of parenting, to her, was letting go, cutting off that umbilical cord that had once connected us as one. She needed to remind herself that letting me "finish becoming who [I was] meant to be" was something she had to do. Our letters showed how we both needed to let the other person know that, despite all our silences and momentary misunderstandings, we really did get each other. When I was younger, my mother used to tell me that even families required a certain amount of yuan, and she had asked me whether I thought the four of us—my parents, my brother, and I—shared yuan. We were sitting on her bed on a Sunday afternoon, after I had distracted her from her studying. I was ten and still possessive of my mother's time whenever I wasn't already busy with something myself. I didn't hesitate for a moment before I answered her and told her that all four of us, without a doubt, shared yuan. There is a Buddhist saying that every child chooses his or her parents. Before a baby is born, it floats in a space between worlds—a space where the baby can "screen" a whole crowd of potential parents and choose a set to whom it wants to belong. When I thought about this theory while working on the baby carrier book with Taichung Ah-ma and my mother, I was convinced that I had chosen to be my mother's daughter.

UMBILICAL CORD

A memory:

It was a Sunday afternoon, and my father and brother were not at home. I had been following my mother around the apartment (a pastime of mine when I was eight years old)—from her bedroom to the kitchen to my father's study and back to her bedroom. Often, I would call out, "Mo-mmy," with an elongated O, insistently interrupting whatever she was doing. When she looked at me and patiently asked, shenme, "What?" I would smile and say, mei you, "Nothing." Sometimes I was embarrassed that I had nothing of import to share, and I was afraid that she would quickly see through my little game of getting her attention. But my mother never failed to stop what she was doing to respond to me. And she never showed disappointment when I offered her the same, uneventful response.

That afternoon, my mother was reading some big book at her desk, which was in one corner of my parents' bedroom. My father had his own separate study with a piano and two dark wood bookcases with glass doors. My mother got a little desk and a skinny section of their bedroom wall for her books. I had been lolling on my parents' bed, at the foot of which was a big mirror. I was intermittently lying down with my head hanging off the edge of the bed and sitting up, watching in the mirror as the blood rushed to my head when I was upside down and the color drained out of my face again when I was right side up.

"Xiao bao," she said suddenly. I stopped making faces at the mirror and tried to look as deserving of her attention as I could. "Come here." She beckoned. I scooted to the corner of the bed and slowly swung my legs out over the edge. I looked up.

"Come," she insisted, "lai, lai." I hopped off the bed and walked over to her chair. "Look!" she said. She opened her palm. In it was a crumpled Chinese envelope, the opening of which was at the short side of the long rectangle. She opened the envelope and shook it over her palm. Out fell what looked like a dried mushroom, all brown and crumbly. I moved closer and breathed into my mother's hand. Some of the looser pieces dangling off the sides quivered in my breath.

"What is it?" I whispered, not realizing that I had moved my hand close to hers. My mother gently wrapped her free hand around mine before I could touch it.

"It's my umbilical cord," she said. And before I could ask her what that was, I looked up and saw that my mother's eyes were brimming with tears. I blinked, and two little teardrops fell from my own eyes and plinked onto my mother's lap, where they made two darkened circles in her pant leg.

"It's the tie between me and my mother," she said. We both looked into her palm at the umbilical cord curled up like a seahorse.

Perhaps it was because I saw the tears in my mother's eyes that, at such a young age, I could see the poetry in that umbilical cord: That something as intangible and complex as the relationship between mother and daughter could be held in someone's hand and kept in an envelope. Certainly part of the reason I cried was that I was jealous and sad. I was jealous that my mother had something so special from her mother; and I was sad that she had not thought to preserve our cord and give it to me as a present.

Whenever I used to complain to my mother that I wished I had been born a genius, she would always say, "Don't worry, you're a late bloomer." Her advice: "Be patient, and don't be lazy."

She had a habit of taking things literally, and it was upsetting to me that she wouldn't even entertain the whimsicality of my imagination. Plus, I never understood how my mother knew things would happen for me later than for others when all the signs pointed to my being an early bloomer, seeing that I had started menstruating in the fourth grade. Even though she was absent (on that business trip in Japan) that dreadful week, I had realized that my girlhood was over; I secretly wished for her to come talk to me—sympathize, the way she so expertly did whenever I was ill—and mourn the loss of my innocence with me. But I took cues from her and from my father's silence and became complicit in the secrecy of my own adolescence. I made my mother promise she would not tell my brother or Meiguo Ah-ma (who was visiting at the time) this dark secret of mine. So the only verbal exchanges we had about my periods were my monthly requests for my mother to buy a pack of sanitary napkins for me. And, as promised, she faithfully—and quietly—bought them and brought the large rectangle of squishy pads to my room, where I could stash them in the innermost corner of my closet.

I know I held my mother most responsible for teaching me that not talking about things was the mature and sensible way to handle situations. When she tucked me into bed, I would try to bring up the thoughts that were swimming furiously in my mind—thoughts about what was happening with my body, about school, my friends, and boys. Always, she made my concerns seem trivial and not worth mentioning. Instead, she pursed her lips, gave me her "you're a late bloomer" speech, told me that the things of real importance would come much later, and pushed my immediate interests aside.

The year I was nine was the same year I began keeping a journal. I began writing with the very conscious intention of remembering what went through my mind at age nine, age ten, age eleven . . . at every age so that I would never forget how to talk to my own daughter when the time came. This was going to be the umbilical cord that would keep me connected to her. I was angry, and now I see that my journals were a symbol of my retaliation against my mother—my resistance to her silencing me.

Another event, which reassured me that my form of silent rebellion was something my mother deserved to suffer:

I used to draw pictures and write poems for my mother. This was a tireless activity with which I busied myself. She and my father worked long hours when their clothing company was still in its beginning stages, and dinners growing up were often a lonely affair involving just me and my brother. After dinner, I would go to my room and spread my Magic Markers and colored pencils out on my desk. Usually, I depicted my mother as a beautiful queen with large, round, sparkling eyes and an upside-down-7 nose, wearing an elaborate gown speckled with gems in all the colors my markers and pencils could combine to make. And the poems were syrupy verses that made use of too many hyperboles, describing how marvelous I knew my mother was. No doubt, I believed my praises and blind devotion were ways to reach her. I left these notes on her pillow. Sometimes, I purposely fell asleep next to these offerings on my parents' bed—how angelic I must look, I thought, sleeping sweetly by these drawings. My mother dedicated an entire drawer to this collection of my drawings and poetry.

One day, I found that the drawer had been emptied.

"Where are my things?" I demanded, shaking the hollow drawer. I still hoarded the gifts I made for my mother as mine. But even so, this possessive display of generosity on my part did not deserve my mother's dismissive reply:

"I threw them away."

She made no attempt to explain herself. She offered nothing to assuage the humiliation of my bruised ego. All I saw was her blank face and became acutely aware of her eyes blinking.

From then on, our relationship began to build itself on silence and tension. I shared little with her, and we exchanged few meaningful words with each other. Meanwhile, I filled journal after journal with an outpouring of unspoken emotion. Soon, of course, the entries were less motivated by the silence that crippled our relationship than by the frivolous desires of a teenage girl. But these were all thoughts—parts of my growing process—to which my mother had no access. She's missing out, I thought to myself—smugly, at first, and then I realized this "victory" came at a great price.

I spent the summer after my freshman year of college at home in Taipei. Some time in July, my mother and I had an argument. It's silly now that I think of it because I can't even remember what we were fighting about, but we spent the rest of my summer vacation at home ignoring each other. It was like a replay of the time I had stopped talking to my father when I was in middle school: As soon as she entered the room, I got up and left. Our apartment was so loaded with the tension that my mother and I fueled with our silence that more than once, my father came into my room and pleaded for me to apologize to my mother, even if she might have been at fault. I apologized to my father instead. "Sorry, Daddy," I said. "I can't do it."

The night before my plane left for New York, I got food poisoning and spent the whole night throwing up. In the morning, my father brought me to the hospital, where the doctor attached the back of my right hand to an I.V. so that I could recover in time to catch my flight. My father came to the hospital, and we said our good-byes there—he had a meeting he had to go to. Someone from his office would take me to the airport. Neither of us mentioned my mother.

Finally, the doctor sent me home to collect my bags. While I was bending over to lock my suitcase, I heard a familiar voice call my name.

"Xiao bao," she said.

I looked up and saw my mother standing in the doorway. Immediately, she blurred into a watery image.

"I'm taking you to the airport," she managed to say before we held each other tightly and cried into one another's shoulders.

Something changed at that moment. On the car ride to the airport, we didn't say much. But in the following school term, the letters between me and my mother flew between New York and Taiwan with a sense of urgency that was yet very new to us. We always wrote each other in Chinese—a promise she had made me keep before sending my brother and me away for summer vacation one year—and we mostly wrote about miscellaneous, mundane things: She gave me reports on everybody's health, described the personalities she met at dinner parties, sent me new strings for the jade necklace she had given me in high school. I wrote her about the time I saw a deer outside my window when I moved out of the dorms and lived in a house with some friends on the edge of a small forest, gave her a list of the classes I was taking at school, sent her a poem I had written for Mother's Day. We were re-introducing ourselves to each other, and though the things we wrote about were often quotidian in nature, it all seemed unbelievably exciting and fascinating. I feel I have missed out on your whole process of growing up, she wrote me once. And I cried when I read that letter.

Years later, when she asked me to collaborate with her on the book about baby carriers, it was only natural to feel the pull between my mother and me become stronger and stronger—a profound closeness that I know we both felt through reading one another's writing, which surfaced only rarely when we were physically together or talking on the phone. Without the medium of writing, our interactions were often slightly awkward—she ended our phone conversations abruptly; I was embarrassed during silences. But alone with her letters and essays, I truly felt—and believed—that aside from Billy, no one else knew me better than my own mother; a realization that was both a relief (I am no longer alone!) and a shock (I am no longer a mystery!).

I have a suspicion that my mother couldn't wait for me to grow up, that she couldn't wait for this precise moment when we could communicate at such a sublimely intimate level. Some people, I have learned, unlearn how to relate to children as soon as they are adults, as soon as they are no longer children themselves. This is perhaps the case with my mother. She threw away my earlier poems and pictures not because she did not appreciate them, but because she couldn't find a real connection to them—a young girl's adoration for her mother was something she took for granted, a natural occurrence that she felt she had not earned herself. What I had remembered as her blank-faced, cruel reply to my asking her what she had down with all my cards and drawings now became an expression that concealed an emotion much more complex and present than I had given her credit for.

I remember now there was an afternoon when I had walked in on my mother crying helplessly on her bed. How big her bed looked with her sitting in the middle of it, her legs bent and swung haphazardly to one side, her body hunched over, shoulders shaking. I was twelve then and still hypersensitive to the realization that parents have real, human emotions. So I began crying harder. My imagination ran wild, fed by the family dramas I tuned into every night at eight—had my parents gotten into a fight? Was there a third party involved? What she actually said to me that afternoon surprised me. I did not understand what she had meant then, but I think I know the source of her frustration now. She said:

"I want to go away for a while. I've been such a terrible mother."

I can't venture to guess precisely what had prompted my mother to feel this way. I can imagine that from time to time, perhaps all mothers feel a certain sense of failure, however unwarranted. We have since never mentioned my stumbling on her crying. She did not end up leaving us. I would like to think that my wrapping my arms around her tightly, howling loudly, "No! you can't! I won't let you!" was what had convinced her to stay. More likely, I know she stayed precisely because she was not a "terrible mother." I understand my mother now in ways I'm not sure she is aware of. We share this secret, encoded language and talk without talking all the time. It is this—this shared lexicon of emotions that is our umbilical cord.

EPILOGUE

The most recent time I went home to Taiwan was for my brother's wedding. I will never forget the look on my father's face when my brother announced, a week after his engagement, that he would get married in Taiwan. Because Alex and his fianceé have been living in Hong Kong for the past six years, we had all assumed that they would get married there. But true to his filial nature, my brother made the decision, I am sure, based on his love and respect for my father and the two starkest differences between weddings in the States and weddings in Taiwan: In Taiwan, weddings are a celebration for the parents (whereas in the States, the focus is almost entirely on the bride and groom), and the groom's side is responsible for the wedding ceremony and banquet (whereas in the States, the bride's side traditionally takes care of the wedding celebrations). My father's eyes lit up and his whole face softened and he seemed to not be able to suppress his smile when my brother made this announcement. I could tell he was so proud of my brother at that moment— proud that he was so understanding of these traditions and that he had made the decision without anyone telling him what he should or should not do. My father had gotten what he silently wanted, and beyond that proud smile, I could see in his melting eyes that he was ready to give my brother anything he wanted in return. It's the kind of face I always imagined my father would have if either of us told him we wanted to move back to Taiwan.

I arrived home one week before the wedding to help with the last-minute preparations. My mother, who had come down with a nasty cold, appeared in high spirits and efficiently relayed to me all the things we still needed to do: Go to a local bakery and buy little pineapple and walnut cakes to put in the out-of-town guests' welcome bags; deliver red envelopes to the chefs at the banquet hall (a traditional formality to "ensure" that the wedding banquet will be as scrumptious as the chefs have promised); and revise the final guest list and seating chart, as it is customary for Taiwanese guests to

RSVP one day before the wedding. On my second day back, I ran these errands with my mom around the city, and from her car window, I peered up at all the new buildings, the latest one being the tallest building in the world (although I knew this record would soon be beaten by some other Asian country, possibly even China), and thought about how quickly the city was progressing, transforming itself. But even with all of Taipei's cutting-edge modernity, I still knew of many more childhood friends who were now opting to move to Shanghai over Taipei.

What Shanghai represents to the Taiwanese today is very similar to what the United States represented to the Taiwanese in the 1970s—opportunity. But the most obvious difference is that the United States also offered an alternative to China's Communist government and a possibility for Taiwan to grow independently from the mainland. An exodus of Taiwanese to Shanghai, however opportune the move would be for Taiwanese businesses because of China's inexpensive cost of labor and living, will only encourage the formation of "one China," in which Taiwan would presumably come under the rule of its motherland. But it is part of the Taiwanese spirit to aggressively seek out business opportunities—especially in the recent economic slump—and even people who were once adamant supporters of Taiwan's independence are now considering the move to cities like Shanghai and Beijing.

At home in Taiwan, I could feel this undeniably palpable excitement in the air—the inevitability of something big about to explode in China—and I could feel the magnetic pull from the mainland, and yes, it did make you want to be there to be a part of it, to get in on it. But politically, it is still difficult to tell what will eventually happen between Taiwan and China. The KMT, the government that is largely responsible for bringing about Taiwan's economic miracle and changing its political structure into a democracy, is the very government that still hopes for reunification with mainland China. The supporters of the DPP, on the other hand, may theoretically stand for Taiwan's independence from the mainland, but when asked and polled, the majority of them still favor the status quo—in which Taiwan is suspended in an international political state of limbo. Many people in Taiwan seem to be unsure, and perhaps they feel that economic stability will somehow guarantee or bring about political stability. Even as I conjure a mental image of Taiwan, the geographical metaphor for its political future is ambiguous—in one view, the tiny, tobacco-leaf-shaped island looks as though it is curled away from the mainland, but in another view, the island leans eagerly toward the motherland.

For many of my uncles and aunts who have spent the past thirty years in the United States—adapting, assimilating, succeeding in their businesses, providing their children with the best educations, and building a close network of friends for themselves—retiring to China is also becoming a viable option. One of my aunts once said to me, "It's strange, after spending the bulk of my life in the United States, I still feel like an outsider. Like I don't fit in." I recalled how much of an outsider I felt my first year in college and multiplied that feeling of loneliness and unbelonging by thirty years. It saddened me to think that thirty-odd years could be temporary—that my uncles and aunts truly emigrated for their children rather than for themselves. For them, I suppose there was always this fantasy of a glorious return home. Perhaps the more difficult realization was that they no longer felt wholly comfortable in Taiwan, either. Indeed, I imagined they felt even more out of place here because Taiwan had changed so dramatically since they'd left. Taiwan was once their home, and it was the place they came from, but now they were more like tourists visiting than natives returning. My parents often introduced their siblings to the latest changes in Taiwanese food, fashion, and even culture, in the same authoritative tone they might explain things to Billy. That's why I could imagine moving to China might grant them the best of both worlds—an environment with familiar customs, language, and food, but that won't constantly remind them of how different the reality of Taiwan is today from that set of nostalgic memories they use for notions of home.

Sitting in the car with my mother, I wondered if I was slowly becoming like my aunts and uncles, having now lived in the States a bit longer than I've spent living in Taiwan (a total of fourteen years in the States and thirteen years in Taiwan). Things were already beginning to seem foreign to me, and my trips home were beginning to feel more and more like short visits, not preparations for my eventual return. As though she were reading my mind (more likely, she noticed the way I was gazing at the passing scenery, as if it were my first time in Taipei), my mother suddenly asked me, "You love

Taiwan, but you don't feel entirely yourself here, do you?"

In the last few years, whenever my mother has asked me about my plans to go back to Taiwan, I have always told her that it was too early to tell and that I hadn't ruled out the idea yet. It was the most diplomatic answer I knew I could give because I was nervous about answering incorrectly. But in truth, I have discovered that I am more at peace with myself when I am not in Taiwan. The only place in Taiwan I feel completely at home is in my parents' house in Tamsui. I love being in my parents' house—it feels like a base, like roots. I know I owe this feeling completely to my mother's attention to detail—the photographs of our family in the living room, the fresh pots of orchids, the paintings my grandfather and I had painted that she framed and hung up on the walls, my brother's old encyclopedia collection still neatly lined up on his shelves, the two altars devoted to my grandfathers. . . . But all this familiarity, this visual display of time and family, has some of the trappings of home, too. When I am in my parents' house, I regress and feel coddled and taken care of and lose my sense of independence and motivation. And when I walk around the streets outside, I feel easily intimidated by the things I no longer know about the city where I grew up. The startling realization is that the disconnect I feel is not only lack of familiarity—for example, no longer knowing which street vendor makes the best egg cakes, or where to go for a good bowl of beef noodle soup, or even how to get from one place to the next on my own, because these are things I could figure out easily and quickly with time. I am now sorely aware of the cultural disjointedness that had always been there (attending an American school in Taiwan, spending summers in the States), but as a young adolescent, I didn't have trouble smoothing over.

"No," I said with measure, "I don't feel completely myself here anymore." My mother looked away. I knew my answer was painful for her to hear, because it was also painful for me to admit. The truth that I will most likely spend the bulk of my life far away from my parents stung like tiny sand particles blown into my eyes.

After a period of silence, she said, almost out of the blue, "You know what kind of bothers me?"

I shook my head.

"When people who left Taiwan a long time ago still keep their citizenship so that they can come back and use our universal health care system because your system in America is so bad. Or other examples like that—people who come back and use Taiwan solely for practical reasons." My mother looked at me with a look of disdain. "I know I shouldn't feel this way, but I do. It just makes this sour feeling in my chest."

I understood perfectly what my mother was saying. But I winced, guiltily wondering whether she felt this same kind of protectiveness over my writing about Taiwan. She hadn't directed her comment toward me, but my own ambivalences—my own tangled, mao dun feelings about home—made me hypersensitive to her resentment toward people whose allegiance and relationship to Taiwan seems so surface.

During the weekend of my brother's wedding, my whole family moved into the hotel where the ceremony and banquet would be held. Alex's wedding day started early—by ten o'clock, my brother, his groomsmen, our extended family, and Billy all gathered in my parents' suite for the traditional tea ceremony, which would officially welcome the bride into our family. My mother was dressed in an antique, dark blue Chinese robe, embroidered with red, yellow, and green flowers and the hems highlighted with metallic threads. My father and brother wore identical black, Chinese-collared jackets that my mother had made for them. Before Alex was to set out for the bridal suite to pick up his bride, he was passed around the room, from my grandmothers to my parents to every uncle and aunt, and listened quietly as they held his hands and gave him some words of advice on marriage and love.

My mother told him that life was like the weather, with unpredictable ups and downs, and that he and his wife had to learn to ride out both the good times and the bad times together. My father glanced briefly at my mother as he told my brother that if he was able to make his wife a happy woman, he would always be a happy man. My aunt who had been there when Alex was born thirty years ago in New York looked at him, and her eyes watered over with tears before she could say one word. My uncles hugged my brother and patted him on the back. My grandmothers, sitting side by side on the couch, spoke in quiet, happy tones, their lips quivering and heads shaking. Somewhere in the back, I could hear my cousin's newborn baby cough in that helpless, endearing way. I looked around the room and felt the distinct euphoric warmth of family, of four generations and many more cultures together in one clear moment of unity. I got a tiny, delicious glimpse into what life could be like if I did live in Taiwan. I thought about the way my mother always speaks about her friends whose sons and daughters have all returned to Taiwan after spending some time living in the States and now have families of their own and, more importantly, kids they are also raising in Taiwan. Like any parent, my mother wants the same thing, and she is jealous of her friends.

I have never told her this, but I am jealous of them, too.

For I, too, have my own fantasies of a glorious return home. But the truth is, I am beginning to feel a much more profound connection to my Americanness. I don't mean that I feel American in a mainstream culture way—I do not know what it feels like to grow up in suburbia or have parents who don't see this country as their true home, and I will never be readily able to sing along to any Billy Joel or Bruce Springsteen song. But I feel American in the "New World," conceptual sense of the word; I feel American precisely because I also feel Taiwanese. While on my trip to China, I couldn't (because I felt I wasn't allowed to) feel a strong connection to my ancestral culture. I can in America because there is the premise of everyone being from someplace else; there is the understanding and freedom for different histories that all journeyed in different ways to continue here. But I know that a large part of why I can feel this way is also because I did not grow up in America. I do not know what it feels like to be made fun of because I come from some place else; I do not know the frustrations of people assuming I can speak Chinese by the way I look, because I can speak Chinese. By the time I came to America, I was seventeen—awkward and still struggling to feel comfortable in my own skin, but already a by-product of multiple cultures, multiple histories, multiple identities.

I must admit that I am often envious of my own parents, whose fierce loyalty to a home—Taiwan—has helped them build a solid foundation for their definition of home. But the truth is, I don't know where I will end up. Most likely, it will not be one place for the rest of my life, as it is for my parents. Most likely, I will always feel a little bit like an outsider wherever I am. When I read that the word "translation" comes etymologically from Latin for "bearing across," it struck a chord with me as I clearly saw the connection between the act of translating—the act of bearing across languages, cultures, and emotional worlds—and the person who translates and, as a result, is translated. That person has an identity that moves across geographical borders, fluidly and sometimes not so fluidly, but always criss-crossing histories, languages, and traditions. For a person who is truly transnational, who is able to adapt relatively easily to any place and situation—perhaps that person's notions of home must be even more distilled and crystallized because home for the translated person is not simply a geographical place or one cultural notion. Home for her is the ribbon of cumulative experiences and memories—an umbilical cord that can never be severed.

ACKNOWLEDGMENTS

This book exists because of the generosity of time and support from many people.

I am grateful to Barbara Lowenstein, Madeleine Morel, and Dr. Phylis Lan Lin because their enthusiasm for my writing and great vision for the manuscript eventually brought this book into being.

I am profoundly indebted to Nancy Agabian, Laura Carden, Catherine Kapphahn, Elizabeth Seay, and Jen Uscher—the women of Six Degrees, whose sensitive and insightful reading helped finesse every draft. I am thankful, as well, for the critiques from early workshops with Nicholas Christopher, Lis Harris, and Richard Locke, who all witnessed the nascent beginnings of a book and encouraged me to follow through on an idea.

Gratitude cannot adequately describe what I feel toward Billy, my better half. He not only read and edited every draft and every fragment of a draft, he talked me through the frustrating lulls of inactivity, stood by me through every humbling experience of rejection, and was there to celebrate every triumph with me, however miniscule or significant. I am deeply grateful for his absolute faith in me, which opened my eyes to possibility and gave me the courage to take risks.

And finally, my utmost appreciation and respect go to my mother, father, and brother for showing me that love and freedom are synonymous.

ABOUT THE
UNIVERSITY OF INDIANAPOLIS PRESS

The University of Indianapolis Press is a nonprofit publisher of original works, specializing in, though not limited to, topics with an international orientation. It is committed to disseminating research and information in pursuit of the goals of scholarship, teaching, and service. The Press aims to foster scholarship by publishing books and monographs by learned writers for the edification of readers. It supports teaching by providing instruction and practical experience through internships and practica in various facets of publishing, including editing, proofreading, production, design, marketing, and organizational management. In the spirit of the University's motto, "Education for Service," the Press encourages a service ethic in its people and its partnerships. The University of Indianapolis Press was institutionalized in August 2003; before its institutionalization, the University of Indianapolis Press published thirteen books, eight of which were under the auspices of the Asian Programs. The Press had specialized in Asian Studies and, as part of its commitment to support projects with an international orientation, will continue to focus on this field while encouraging submission of manuscripts in other fields of study.

BOOKS FROM THE
UNIVERSITY OF INDIANAPOLIS PRESS
(1992–2003)

1. Phylis Lan Lin, Winston Y. Chao, Terri L. Johnson, Joan Persell, and Alfred Tsang, eds. (1992) *Families: East and West.*

2. Wei Wou (1993) *KMT-CCP Paradox: Guiding a Market Economy in China.*

3. John Langdon and Mary McGann. (1993) *The Natural History of Paradigms.*

4. Yu-ning Li, ed. (1994) *Images of Women in Chinese Literature.*

5. Phylis Lan Lin, Ko-Wang Mei, and Huai-chen Peng, eds. (1994) *Marriage and the Family in Chinese Societies: Selected Readings.*

6. Phylis Lan Lin and Wen-hui Tsai, eds. (1995) *Selected Readings on Marriage and the Family: A Global Perspective.*

7. Charles Guthrie, Dan Briere, and Mary Moore. (1995) *The Indianapolis Hispanic Community.*

8. Terry Kent and Marshall Bruce Gentry, eds. (1996) *The Practice and Theory of Ethics.*

9. Phylis Lan Lin and Christi Lan Lin. (1996) *Stories of Chinese Children's Hats: Symbolism and Folklore.*

10. Phylis Lan Lin and David Decker, eds. (1997) *China in Transition: Selected Essays.*

11. Phylis Lan Lin, ed. (1998) *Islam in America: Images and Challenges.*

12. Michelle Stoneburner and Billy Catchings. (1999) *The Meaning of Being Human.*

13. Frederick D. Hill. (2003) '*Downright Devotion to the Cause': A History of the University of Indianapolis and Its Legacy of Service.*

For information on the above titles or to place an order, contact:
University of Indianapolis Press
1400 East Hanna Avenue / Indianapolis, IN 46227 USA
(317) 788-3288 / (317) 788-3480 (fax)
lin@uindy.edu / http://www.uindy.edu/universitypress

NEW TITLES FROM THE
UNIVERSITY OF INDIANAPOLIS PRESS
(2004–2005)

1. brenda Lin. *Wealth Ribbon: Taiwan Bound, America Bound.*

2. May-lee Chai. *Glamorous Asians: Short Stories and Essays.*

3. Chiara Betta. *The Other Middle Kingdom: A Brief History of Muslims in China* (in Chinese and English). Translated by Phylis Lan Lin and Cheng Fang.

4. Phylis Lan Lin and Cheng Fang. *Operational Flexibility: A Study of the Conceptualizations of Aging and Retirement in China* (in Chinese and English). Translated by Phylis Lan Lin and Cheng Fang.

5. Alyia Ma Lynn. *Muslims in China* (in Chinese and English). Translated by Phylis Lan Lin and Cheng Fang.

6. Philip H. Young. *In Days of Knights: A Story for Young People.*

7. James C. Hsiung. *Comprehensive Security: Challenge for Pacific Asia.*

8. Winberg Chai. *Saudi Arabia: A Modern Reader.*

9. Au Ho-nien. *Journey with Art Afar.* Catalog for the Au Ho-nien Museum, University of Indianapolis.